Apprenticeship of The Soul

Sonjan

Fana Press
Post Office Box 1
Orcas Island, WA 98280

Apprenticeship of The Soul

Copyright © 2011 by D. Christopher McCombs

Published by:
Fana Press
Post Office Box 1
Orcas Island, Washington 98280
fana@rockisland.com   (360) 392-8003

Hardcover: ISBN 13: 978-1-893486-12-6 * ISBN 10: 1-893486-12-5
Tradepaper: ISBN 13: 978-1-893486-10-2 * ISBN 10:1-893486-10-9

Cover painting by Greg Spalenka

Author contact:
PO Box 1, Orcas Island, WA, 98280
sonjan@rockisland.com

Library of Congress Control Number: 2011930568

Publisher's Cataloging-in-Publication data:

Sonjan, Chris McCombs
Apprenticeship of The Soul
ISBN   978-1-893486-10-2   [1-893486-10-9]

1. Consciousness. 2. Spiritual life. 3. Poetry 4. Self-actualization. 5. Self perception. 6. Change. 7. Self-evaluation. 8. Psychology. 9. Inspiration.10. Title.

Dedicated to

The Blue Star Mother

Immortal Master of the Solar Lineage

Also by the Author

Delicious Silence:
poems from the tiger's mouth

ISBN 1-893486-08 7

Beloved:
love poems to the Holy One

ISBN 1-893486-08-7

www.fanapress.com
360.390.5449

Table of Contents

Sonjan

For years I avoided spiritual names. I didn't want
an India-sounding name. I had friends who took
Sanskrit names and they always felt contrived.
Besides, my existing names were beautiful. David
meant beloved of God and Christopher meant the
bearer of Christ. Those were first-class spiritual
names in my book. And I had always liked last
name of McCombs. It was a strong Scottish name.

Then I met Steve Gray at the Inner Dimensions
Conference in 2001. I felt an immediate affinity
with his luminous heart. He was the unknown
speaker at the conference. He shared his personal
story with me of studying Zen Buddhism for years
and at the request of his teacher, began to teach.
His teachings were well attended locally.

Then he gave himself a spiritual name —
Adyashanti — and the rest is history. In that
moment I released my judgment of spiritual
names.

Names carry vibration. Spiritual names are meant
to express a "quality of being" and draw us towards
their essence. Spiritual names can change as we
deepen and mature or stay for a lifetime.

Padmasambhava was said to have nine names
before the Tibetans honored him as the lotus born.

During a healing seminar in '06, my friend and mentor Aaravindha offered to enter Divine Mind through his gift of *saumedhika* sight and pull out a spiritual name from the Mother's heart for me. That name is Sonjan. It means gentle heart.

This book is the collected teachings of Sonjan. It embodies forty years of study, meditation and spiritual practice. It is the knowledge of a lifetime. I offer it to you.

Foreword
by Aaravindha Himadra*

Sonjan's search for the eternal is palpable in the inspiring verses of his poetry. His heartfelt words are filled with joy, revelation, and the epiphanies of a life lived in spiritual fervor, love for the divine, and a deep compassion for the thirsting soul. Our troubled world desperately needs the kind of spiritually oriented optimism that Sonjan puts forward so lovingly in this book.

Sonjan's poetry reminds us of our shared mystical journey, through providing a first hand look at his life-changing discoveries on the light-strewn path to illumination. Reading his words, one is moved by his devotion and passion for gathering and distilling the intricate threads of wisdom that weave us together as the divine children of one eternal Being. His poems are a journey of the heart, eloquently revealing the depth of his faith in a way that anyone can easily feel and appreciate.

Sonjan combines the familiar perspective of a householder with the passionate devotion of a true mystic. This is an important precedent for our world today. All too often, the kind of sacred concepts infused into his poems are entrusted solely to the impassioned spirit-hungry monk or sadhu.

And yet, to a great extent, Sonjan's ability to gently bridge the two worlds, through his well-earned knowledge of both realms, is exactly what our new humanity is calling out for today. Our world is hungry for a new language, one that speaks to all people, regardless of their spiritual denominations, or lack thereof.

In truth, all beings thirst for a knowledge that sets them free. Sonjan's book is a step in that direction, through which the playful and kind language of his heart transcends the boundaries which separate the many diverse seekers in this world. Sonjan offers them a taste of the sweetness of truth. It neither judges or condemns, but rather uplifts and revels in the possible.

This inspirational collection of poems echoes many of the most important eye-opening moments that lead to the realization of one's essential divinity. It chronicles many of Sonjan's personal trials and ecstasies of his own journey. His generous insights are intended as both support and guidance for all those sincere beings who have already, or will one day, set out on the mystical path, in hope of awakening their spiritual empowerment and realizing their Self-liberation.

*Aaravindha bio located in back of book

Introduction
by Sonjan

An inspired poem writes itself. It comes from beyond the mind. It arrives as a field of information embedded within energy that unfolds into impressions.

Describing the process is difficult. Some call it channeling. Others use terms like "vesseling the Spirit". I call it inspiration. It just happens. It's what creative artists do. It is opening to the energy and letting it inform you. Perhaps it's a dimensional opening or simply the rational left brain opening to the intuitive right hemisphere or both.

In either case, a door simply opens and in comes an energy, rich in a non-rational, non-linear flow of information. You read the energy and translate it into your craft.

These poems began in meditation. I had been given a book of Rumi poems in the mid 90's. The fusion of profound wisdom, intimacy with God and wild metaphor broke me open. I read everything Coleman Barks had written. Then Hafiz arrived on the wings of Daniel Ladinsky's gifted pen. I knew these men. They were my intimates, my teachers, my friends. They laid me wide open. I read and re-read until, one day during meditation, the pen leaped into my hand and began writing poems. The portal simply opens; I stop everything and write. That's how it happens for me.

My first two books were published in 2000 and a book of love poems followed. My focus then shifted from poetry to home, garden and lover, in what I now call 'the home and garden years' — good for flowers, not so good for poems. A sort of poetic ice age settled in for the next five years as I grew roses.

The poems began again in '06 when I began working with Aaravindha, an American born mystic. The creative doors flung open and the poems in this book began to write themselves.

They represent the emerging wisdom of the Solar Lineage, mixed with the wisdom of a lifetime, the fusion of a dozen traditions distilled in the fire of a human life. I hope you enjoy them.

The Idea of
Commentary & Personal Perspective

Commentary

The poems are accompanied by commentary, intended to add depth and perspective to what the poem attempts to say. Context can frame a poem and provide insight that the poem itself may not embody. That is the beauty of the prose-poetry fusion.

The poem can fly, revealing the flow of feeling, metaphor and intuitive insight. An inspired poem can take you where the mind cannot go.

Commentary grounds that flow in the conceptual mind, giving meaning and understanding — an important marriage.

Personal Perspective

My perspective deepens when artists share what is happening with them as they paint the painting or write the song. It is in this spirit that I have included a very personal perspective in the form of notes woven throughout the commentary.
I want to share with you the personal aspect of the poems, I want to let you in on the process, how they came about, what was going on, what was emerging. I hope you enjoy this added thread.

Each poem notes the date it was written so you can sense the evolving adventure of the process.

Poems first, commentary second

I suggest you read the poem first — on the right side page — then go to the left facing page to read the commentary. That allows for the experience to arise first and lets conceptual understanding follow.

What is Enlightenment?
by Sonjan

What is enlightenment? There is deep misunderstanding on the topic. Is enlightenment the same as self-realization? Is it the same as self-recognition? Are there degrees of it? What are the attributes?

When I first heard of enlightenment, I assumed it to be the omega point of the human experience. My mind imagined that the individual nature improves and improves until some superlative state was achieved. As a seeker, I assumed it to be a point far off in the future, perhaps lifetimes away.

Does anyone get enlightened? Not in the sense that the question is asked. Enlightenment is not the separate self becoming the biggest, baddest, wisest, separate self on the block. That never happens. The separate self never gets enlightened. The mind never gets enlightened.

In enlightenment, the separate self opens to the larger transpersonal, unified Oneness that is its source and essence. The separate self opens and allows a larger pre-existing awareness that was always there but had gone unnoticed and unrecognized, to enter and become it, hence the name self realization or self recognition. What you thought in the beginning was separate turns out not to be so separate, but that is a recognition that comes with realization.

I like the metaphor of "the point and the field". The field is the unified transpersonal awareness that contains all the points with in It (God). All points exist within the field. Each point is a part of the field, not the entire field, but a valid perspective within the field. While the point and the field are distinct, are they separate? No, they are the same, and when the point opens to the field, that becomes self-evident.

When we start the journey towards enlightenment, many assume that the journey involves "who-we-think-we-are" to move from the alpha to the omega point. When we get there we are enlightened. But this is a false model. Enlightenment happens when the point finally opens to the field. The field floods in and the point is no longer separate from the field, yet it is still a distinct point of view within the field.

The metaphor has many wonderful subtleties, but the essence is that enlightenment is not an acquisition, a state or an improvement of the separate self, but the releasing of the identity as a separate self long enough for your colorless, odorless, tasteless, soundless unattributed essential consciousness to recognize Itself as who you really are. That takes OPENING.
So, throughout the entire book, you hear the theme repeating: open, open, open.

People ask their teachers "Are you enlightened?" My feeling is that it is the question you don't ask. If you want to know, you are probably asking from a place of separation. A deeper question to ask yourself might be: "Who is asking?" If the person claims, "I am enlightened. I am enlightened." the odds are that they too are coming from the perspective of separate self. However, to say, "No, I am not enlightened," affirms separation, which is also misleading. Ramana Maharshi is often quoted as saying, "The thought that you are not enlightened, is the biggest obstacle to your enlightenment."

Besides, the Ministry of Magic does not send you a Certificate of Enlightenment by owl mail when self-realization occurs. Eckhart sat on a park bench for two years. Byron Katie had to develop "the work" to heal her crazy mind.

Susan Segal reported in Collision With The Infinite that she wandered around for ten years after her awakening not knowing what happened to her as she stepped on that bus. And, by the way, if you do get a letter by owl after your awakening, please contact me; maybe my owl went missing.

"As the ego approaches the Divine

It dissolves like sugar in water"

You Are What Is pg 287

Not That Kind of Poet
10-1-07

I am not the "remembering" kind of poet
I can't quote Yeats or Shelley
Or the brilliance of Shakespeare
I can't even remember my own material

But there is wildness afoot
A madness that comes visiting when you let go

Rumi's heart fell to the ground when he lost Shams
Then the Divine came and danced
Until his mouth became a blessing
God wrote a thousand poems to Himself on his tongue

The wildness that ripped Hafiz apart
Comes visiting
She rips me open — grabs a pen
And starts scribbling Divine madness

I am not the remembering kind of poet
I'm not really a poet at all
I'm just crazy about kissing God

Commentary: The Great Effort

This is the paradigm shift from struggle to effortlessness. When ego opens to the Divine, then Life begins working on your behalf. For the first time, effortlessness becomes possible. You no longer force your way through the universe. Creation acts on your behalf, because you are the universe.

These were the first lines of a long poem. But then, the pen stopped. Nothing more could be added. The truth had landed.

The Great Effort
10-10-08

Struggle is a clever disguise
For resisting the truth

Effort is the depth
Of your commitment to struggle

Lack is the fruit you bare
For making love with such scoundrels

Commentary: Separation Leaves You Blind

This short poem expresses a theme that will be presented throughout the book. It will be expanded upon, reiterated, and investigated from different angles. The theme is simple: separation from God leaves you blind.

The poem uses the Sufi convention of including the poet's name in the poem. Hafiz and Jeshua were whispering in my ear in this poem.

Separation Leaves You Blind
3-30-06

Why is it
That God is so hard to find
So easy to miss?

Here's Sonjan's idea:

Any thought that you are separate from Love
Or any thought that you are separate from God
Closes the eyes
And leaves you blind

Commentary: Your Pilot

Your Pilot is an intimate discussion between the God that incarnates as Soul, and the part that stays behind as Source, regarding what is about to happen. It reveals the willingness of the Soul to incarnate, knowing full well that it will get crushed. It does this out of love, so that this dimension can be perceived by the Source and the Soul can actualize the wisdom, love and power of its own Divine Nature.

This poem was written in the Hilo airport after it had just rained four feet in four days and the island of Hawaii was under water in a state of emergency. But the airport was comfortable and charming. People were reading, talking on their cell phones, working on their laptops.

I sat down, the door opened, and the Divine was whispering in my ear. I reached for my yellow pad and for an hour, page after page came through, as if Hafiz himself were giving me line after line. Tears were streaming down my face and my heart was openness itself. It was an intense experience. At the end lay this poem, *Your Pilot*.

Your Pilot
1-27-08

I will be Your pilot
I will be Your first seat
Will operate this vehicle
I will perceive for You

But You, Beloved
Must navigate

I will come on Your adventure
Take a body and fall into the flesh
I will dream the dream for You
I will miss You in my bones

But You, Beloved, must navigate for us
Don't let me forget — don't let me forget
 "But sweetheart, forgetting is the plan"
And I fell and fell and fell until I forgot

Now, I call out to You in pain
Asking why You cast me out

CONTINUED >>

When the pain is too great — I die
You send me back again

When I cry out, You whisper in my ear
 "There is a better way, sweetheart"
But I will not hear You
For I will have suffered the forgetting

When my bottom, built by suffering, fully forms
I will have tired of this pain — I will open to
Another way, not knowing what that is
Though those still suffering will deny it

I will roll my head back, looking up
To where I imagine You are
And cry out . . . "I surrender"
I will admit I have made a mess of it

I will admit that I am lost in Your duality, that
I don't know how to behave in Your playground
I will admit that I have listened to my mind
Until bruised and battered

You will whisper, so softly in my ear
"Stay at the wheel, sweetheart
I will be your navigator."

You will take my hand in Yours
And teach me to listen
You will teach me to hear my own Heart

You will show me how my negative focus
Always dragged me down
How resistance always failed me

You will share Your secrets with me
The power of awareness
The wisdom of allowing
The blessing of gratitude

I will become skillful within the mind
Creating deliberately, effortlessly
You will then lift my sights beyond the mind
Introduce me to silence and
The awareness that lives there

CONTINUED >>

In the silence — I will finally meet You
Invisible, beyond sense perception
The ultimate perceiver, pure consciousness
Not different than my own Divine Self

We will laugh together at this outrageous adventure
Where what we were looking for
Was who was looking
You sought Yourself outside of Yourself
Not knowing that You were the treasure

But now I know — that we are not two
That it is You looking out these eyes
You, kissing with these lips
Giving Yourself to the world which is also You

Now I know
That there is only God
That there is only You
And that everyone and everything is That

The World Does Not Want Lovers
11-15-07

The world does not want poets and lovers
Too much life, too much exuberance
The mind wants structure and continuity

It wants accountants and builders
Warriors and religions — it wants FORM
The mind doesn't really even like Life
It's too wild, too messy and unpredictable

Life disrupts: it builds; then tears down
Then builds again
It's just too ALIVE for the mind

The world wants predictability
But Life and Love come running naked
Through the manicured landscape
And set it all on fire

Life is a passionate dance
Between form and consciousness
Structure and love
Both requiring the other

Commentary: She Feeds Me

There are a dozen poems from 2000, which were written after the earlier books went to press. They reflect the pure "not-two" perspective that was so alive for me. Poems like *She Feeds Me* and *Broken Open* reflect this constant opening-opening-opening and the bliss that comes with it.

In the final stanza of *She Feeds Me*, the gift is being offered with the admonition that the journey from ego to Essential Nature requires releasing an erroneous, yet cherished, identity.

Yes, the caterpillar can fly, but not until it lets go of its identity and allows a complete restructuring. From the perspective of an unwilling identity, that feels like being torn apart, like death itself.

She Feeds Me
6-10-2000

I am in love
With the Holy One
Night and day
Her love feeds me

One afternoon
She asked me to show you the way
To this river of wine

My friend, I have a gift for you
If you don't mind being torn apart

Commentary: Broken Open

Broken Open uses the metaphor of the egg to get at the ego issue. The shell, representing ego, has a wonderful purpose, but also its limitations.

If the shell does not yield, does not crack open to the emerging chick, then there is no further Life, no further development. The poem uses this simple metaphor and applies it to the ego identity as it "cracks open" to the emerging Spirit.

Broken Open
6-18-2000

The pathway to God
Is the heart
Broken open

The shell is needed
For the chick to grow
But then — it must crack open

Commentary: Free, But Not Satisfied

This is a love poem to you who have been on the path for a lifetime, for those who were bitten early, for senior students and devoted teachers, for those who have made it to the gates of freedom, either inside or out.

When my dharma brother, David Lear, shared his story of doing 100,000 full body prostrations as part of the preliminary ngöndro practice of the Vajrayana Buddhist tradition, my heart went out to all of us who have been "at this" for lifetimes, certainly this lifetime. I call it walking to Lhasa on your knees. I felt compassion for all of us "doing practice" or the non-practice of inquiry, or India or whatever. So much awareness has gone into sadhana, realization and polishing the stone.

At some point you had your breakthrough, the core experience of Self, or you left the monastery, as goes the story of the sixth patriarch, only to find your illumination with a courtesan in the village.

For those who have quieted the mind, discovered silence and are sitting in stillness dissolved into your Divine Nature; I salute you. You have found your freedom. But are you yet a free bird?

As delicious as silence is and as wonderful as stillness is, there is more. And if you have been sitting in silence for years, you most certainly have heard the call.

All realization must be actualized. It must be lived and integrated throughout all the bodies. For that you must step back into life, into the power of creation and sing your dharma song. The cave will not fulfill you even if it's in Mill Valley.

Free, But Not Satisfied
6-15-08

What is the point?
You ask.
You thought thirty years of practice
Would free you from this cage

Yet here you are — stuck in silence
Nowhere to go, not really fulfilled
You made it to the top of the mountain, you thought
Having recognized your Self as silence

That should have done it
But you are not yet a free bird
Why not?
Silence has become a cage

So many beautiful souls
Have come out of the temples
Casting off their robes
To stand with the people

Your fate is not
To dissolve into silence
Though blissful
Silence is unfulfilling

Your job is to LISTEN
To what silence wants to bring forth
To uplift an aching world

You cannot grasp Totality
It's too much for the mind
But you can feel the radiance
Shining through the Ocean

Listen — for the Shine
Flowing through silence
That vast intelligence is offering Herself
As the answer

This dance troupe you have joined
Has an asymmetry to it called time
The oscillating poles of duality
Create an ongoing need

CONTINUED >>

Every need summons an answer
The Shine is here to answer that need

You who have awakened within the dream
Are the ones who can answer
Who can listen for and hear
The divine order

Don't just sit there
Silence is asking you
To listen for the divine intention
Begging to be expressed

Yes, you can take the position
That it's all perfect just as it is
That there is no "you" to do anything anyway

But the Mother is whispering in your ear
And She will not leave you alone, until you listen
Until then, you will feel unfulfilled

Silence allows listening
Beyond the clatter of separation
But silence is more than a noun

Silence is the medium
Through which Divine Intelligence
Summons the solution from within Itself
To order a chaotic world

You who have awakened
Are Her champions
Break free, listen
Become salve to this world

Commentary: The Animal

This is a poem about integration. It stands in contrast to the medieval idea of debasement of the flesh. It presents the contradiction that you are both the transcendent Divine AND the individualized self at the same time.

I wrote the poem during a time when my own animal was strong and I was being challenged to integrate.

The animal is the body and the energy that comes with it, both divine and individual. Yes, you are the body, but also not limited to the body. It is your instrument of expression.

The Animal
7-26-08

Until your animal is sacred
You will wander this world

Until your Spirit and your animal lie down together
Until your vitality and your Essential Nature
Become lovers, forgetting all distinctions
Until then, there will be no lasting peace
There will be roaming, and searching, and becoming

But when your Divine Self and your individuation
Become One, then you are whole
Then you can walk this world as your Self
Then, you ARE the great mystery

Being and becoming become One
The local and the non-local no longer bicker
The Transcendent and the individuation
Will be realized — to be the same thing

Essence expressing Itself

Commentary: The Steering Wheel

Surrendering to your own listening can disappoint others. It can even disappoint your own mind.
I wrote this as I was ending a relationship.

Are you surrendered to the truth? Then what can you say, but the truth?

The Steering Wheel
1-8-09

I finally stopped
Ripping the steering wheel
From the Mother's hands
Demanding "My will be done"

I have, too long, skinned my knees
And broken my bones singing that song
Now, I am interested
In what She has to say

What do You want, Sweetheart?
What adventure are You interested in today?
What slice of perfection
Needs expression now?

No resistance to the truth
Leaves your heart undefended
Singing Her beautiful song
From your sweet lips

Commentary: The Royal Road

The Royal Road expresses the complete delight that awaits us just beyond the mind, if we have the courage to make the journey.

The Royal Road
6-6-2000

Vulnerability
Opens the gate to grace

This is the royal road
Crying out for God
Asking for help
Longing for union

Come on your knees
Crying , weeping
Be that vulnerable
That broken open

You think
You are being thrown down
But longing is the sound
Of being lifted up

Commentary: Called Into Darkness

This is a creation poem. It summarizes the human experience in eight lines. It is a precursor to longer, more descriptive poems on the topic, Poems like *The Big Lie* and *The Vulnerability of God* present the whole story in a more narrative style.

Called Into Darkness is very concise, very Zen. I love this style. It says the most with the least. The economy of it reminds me of Dogen's famous poem*:

> Midnight. No waves,
> No wind, the empty boat
> Is flooded with moonlight

* quoted by Stephen Mitchell, from The Enlightened Heart, Harper-Perennial, p 49

Called Into Darkness
6-30-2000

We are called into darkness
We get crushed
Then we hear
The call Home

That's the way it is
With human beings
That is how coal
Becomes a diamond

The Ice Age and Beyond

The poetry door seemed to close after 2000
and stayed closed for five years. I built a house
and adventured in home and garden with my
sweetheart. I studied how creation forms, how
to manifest reality. Could it truly be done from
effortlessness? I was no longer interested in
forcing, but could manifestation really be done
effortlessly? The results were impressive and I
did well during these years. But my focus was
about to deepen again.

I began *A Course in Miracles* in 2006. The course
is a remarkable teaching with a huge perspective.
I love its focus on forgiveness and non-separation.
You can hear it in poems like *Separation Leaves
You Blind* and *When the Mind Stops Whining*. I also
began working with Aaravindha that year. The door
of inspiration opened again and the poems
re-emerged.

The 2006 poems reflect the fusion of the Course's
emphasis on forgiveness and non separation,
Ramana Maharshi's inquiry, which had been
maturing for a dozen years, and my growing
understanding of the Solar Lineage focused on
Life, listening and divine intention. All of this was
wrapped in the divine intimacy of those marvelous
Sufi poets, Rumi and Hafiz.

By 2007 the fusion was complete. I was deeply involved with Aaravindha's teachings, and my life was changing.

A dynamic transforming force is at work with the Solar Lineage masters. You can feel it. It changes your life. My focus on home and garden ended. My seven-year love relationship was over. My focus shifted towards giving back. I began listening for the need in the moment.

The '07 and '08 poems reflect the deepening. Poems like *The Vulnerability of God* express the deep esoteric perspectives that were emerging from divine mind through Aaravindha's *saumedhika* sight.

Commentary: The Vulnerability of God

The Vulnerability of God is a teaching poem. It
came as a response to the impassioned question
of WHY?   Why do we exist? Why are we
here? Why is there so much suffering? I had
watched the angst of a woman as she cried out
to understand. Is there a divine plan? Is there
any purpose to this life at all? I could hear the
profound frustration in her voice.

I wanted to take her aside and share what I had
learned over a lifetime. But the shift from the
common view to a deeper understanding involves
the unraveling of deeply held beliefs. So answering
the question of "why" may take some time.

The Vulnerability of God tracks the tapestry of
existence. We weave together the fall into flesh,
the crushing of innocence, the bottom, the search,
the empowerment and the realization.

It is something to chew on, something to challenge
your beliefs, something for you to consider. I am
inviting you into an investigation. I am inviting you
to listen. Use your intuitive discrimination
to determine what is true.

The Vulnerability of God
7-6-08

The vulnerability of God is this:
When God enters duality — Oneness is forgotten
Do you remember who you are?
Where you came from? How you got here?

The power you and God gain
Through this adventure in separation is — remembering
You are forced to remember who you are
Because that is the true seat of your power

That is where you find the sweetness, the effortlessness
You assumed God was perfect
And in Oneness that is true
But here in creation, God enters and gets crushed

God enters with innocence, but that innocence is naïve
And, as yet, lacks the power and wisdom Of Its own Essence
So, Oneness enters duality where the powerful
Dominate the weak — and innocence is crushed

CONTINUED >>

But out of the ashes of that crushing a bottom forms
The incarnating Soul finally says: ENOUGH ! ! !
In the midst of the suffering the Soul cries out:
"There must be a better way!" and the search begins

In the beginning
We don't know what we are looking for
What we are searching for
We just know — there has to be more to it than survival

Until that bottom forms there is not much you can do
It's the free fall of innocence
But the bottom does form and it can form anywhere
Some bottoms are more graceful than others

This is the price God pays
To play within His kingdom
This is the price of relationship
This is the price of TWO

The search for a better way winds across millennia
Through triumph and failure, from path to path
Then, somewhere, you catch the scent of your Self
Your divine Self, and the pace quickens

You find your way to the first realization:
I am That — I am That — you realize in the silence
You have freed yourself from the tonnage of
Misidentification, but you still have kleshas*
Your mind still obstructs

That is where you come to know that you are Divine
And that it is simply the mind that needs healing

Now you are at base camp, which happens to be at
21,000 feet. The air is so rarified here
That only the devoted and the lucky
Have made it this far

The ascent to the top is before you
You begin healing your mind
From every insanity you picked up
Along your noble way

Here, you will meet a true teacher
Who will unlock the door to the Light
For it is the Light that does the work on this path
It is the Light that heals the mind

CONTINUED >>

* Kleshas are vulnerabilities that allows unconscious negative
patterns to express

There are masters along this way
Waiting to help you
Reach out to them
They are your brothers

And it is their great honor to grasp your hand in theirs
And give you a leg up
You are soooo close to Home now
That you can smell the sea air — the scent of Light

Bliss filled
You reach out to others
And find that you are the helping hand
You reached for

Put the Book Down
a note on reading poetry

If you are touched or moved by the poems, then
put the book down for a moment and enjoy that
feeling. That feeling is more important than
reading.

Poems can inspire. They can take us to the place
where the poet drew his inspiration. A heart poem
can take us into our hearts. I wrote these poems to
help lift you up your vibration tree, to offer insight
as to what might be right around the corner for
you.

I am with you on this journey — right here with
you, igniting the flames of passion for the sacred.
This is our collective journey. I am here to help you
fly. Nothing would please me more than to see your
wings grow and watch you ascend in the flight of
the swan.

Poetry is for savoring.

Commentary: Swan Born

I wrote this poem for the lovers of God, the bhaktis, for those who have been blessed with devotion to the Divine. It is full of affection for those who have been on the path for a very long time.

The call is given: Come pick up your power and be a divine participant in the Mother's great adventure of creating paradise. Roll up your sleeves and get involved in listening for and expressing the Divine Intention rolling thunderously through silence.

All realization has to be actualized.

Swan Born
6-21-08

Come, sweet beauties
Meditators, yogis, lovers and seekers
You who have walked to Lhasa on your knees
Meditated a lifetime, sought the Kingdom in a
Thousand ways

You who have fallen in love with silence
And adore the Holy One
Listen, just listen
There is an impulse moving through silence

It's ringing in your heart
It is the power of God knocking from the inside

There is a Divine Order moving through time
Do you hear it? It is just beyond your ears
It is calling you to become your Self
To be the winged creature that you are

CONTINUED >>

Let that impulse fill your wings

Address the need
Arising in this moment
To express the Mother's love
The Father's wisdom

You, who are swan born
Came to this world for this
You came here, just for this

This is the Gift
11-3-07

This is the gift I came to give
To meet your Self
And know it for the first time
To rest in the silence and know it to be your Self

To be free of running
From what can never go away

Commentary: Love Rules

If *Called Into Darkness* has the economy of Zen, then *Love Rules* has the overflowing love heart of the Sufi poets, like Hafiz. It is a raucous poem, full of life. It danced off my pen in about two minutes.

Can you hear the mixing flavors of *A Course in Miracles* with the Sufi metaphor?

Love Rules
3-23-06

Love rules !!!
Love wants to dance
To tango across the floor of Life
As if nothing else mattered

To tear off Her clothes
And make wild wanton love to Life

Love wants to extend Herself
Into every corner of your mind
Until each thought surrenders
Saying "I give. I give"

Until every thought admits
That the tiny-mad-idea of separation from God
Was a reeeeally bad idea
And gets their tail back home to Love

Any idea of separation
Breaks the wine glass

Commentary:
Paradise is Letting Her Become You

I wrote this to tell her that she was the Divine
herself. When she smiled the whole room lit up.
When she spoke, it was music.

When she came in that morning and said,
"I realize that I am the silence." She was the
Goddess Herself speaking. I wanted to hug her
forever, to acknowledge that moment of awakening.

Hugging her changed my life.

Paradise is Letting Her Become You
12-16-07

Look no further, beloved
You are the body of heaven
The wings of the Mother
The soft body of paradise

Both the creator and creation
The singer and the song
The pitcher and the clear water within

Why dream of separation
 When your smile turns lead into gold
You open to Her and out of your mouth come pearls
You surrender and She is looking out your eyes

Paradise
Is letting Her become you

Commentary: Divine Nuisance

I was having a day of bliss. The Mother had opened the portal and my heart flew out Her window. This playful poetry came through. My pen would not stop writing. She was playing with me through the poetry. The poem began as my voice, but somewhere changed to Hers. She was making fun of the linear mind and splashing around in Sufi metaphor. My pen was flying.

In the last stanza, She turns to the conundrum, giving away what can't be given.

Divine Nuisance
7-25-07

Ahhh . . . BLISS . . . my courtesan, my companion
The blood in my veins
Sought in all worlds, but found only in the Heart
I found her years ago in meditation

What a blessed day that was
Then I chased her for decades
Until the Friend said
 "Bliss is the radiance, not the cause.
Find out who you are. Find out who is looking"

And I was freed from that search
Now She flows in my veins, a companion to Herself
Free of searching. Free to give back
Free   to DANCE

You have touched the Poet within
Now everything is verse
Prose took the day off and only poems flow

CONTINUED >>

Only clothes left strewn on the floor trace the path
To the luminous door my Heart just flew out
She could be off dancing for days

I love it when the Poet shows up
And claims my mouth as Her own
 Driving all linear thoughts from the house
Only verse will do today — what a blessing

The book will read beautifully, intelligently
Building to lucid conclusions, then poetry breaks
Loose and dancing, partying, and music arrive
Her stockings hanging from the crown

Joy has broken free, dances across my chest
It can go on like this for pages
Before I return to my senses
And the lucid clarity of thought

People will ask, "What just happened, Sonjan?"
And I'll say, "Talk to the Blue Star Mother
She just opened my heart and the poet leapt out

Now he's running around town
Being a divine nuisance."

Where is joy found?
In giving back what can't be given

"Creation is a physical projection

Of what is inside your mind

If you work it solely from the outside

The weird failures never end"

Weird Failures pg 113

Commentary: Faith

This is a statement of what faith means. The word is often misused to mean strong belief, but faith has nothing to do with belief.

I wanted to clearly say what I meant when I used the word. The essence of faith is surrender.

Faith
10-10-08

You can run and you can hide.
You can scheme and be clever
But always, there you are
A "you" struggling, searching

What if it were easier than that?
What if it were so simple that you'd missed it?

There is another path open to us, called faith
Faith has nothing to do with belief
Faith is surrendering your fears and hopes
To the Divine Life flowing through you

What if you gave up all resistance
To the way things were
And became interested in the truth

What if you became defenseless
To your own Divine Nature?

CONTINUED >>

Could you ask, instead of struggle?
Could you listen, instead of react?
What would it be like to be on the side
Of your own Deepest Self, wanting what It wanted?

The mind is an instrument, not a sovereign
It is designed to serve the Spiritual Heart

Which side do you want to be on?

"I open my heart — you fill it with love

I ask a question — you put the answer in my mouth

I summon you — love overwhelms me

Now, even my foolishness

wants to come see you"

Blue Star Mother pg 295

Commentary: Who Are You, Really?

This is aimed at the heart of the identity issue. It takes the issue head on: to correct the day-to-day ordinary misidentification with mind. Who are you?

The mind will insist on referencing its own identity as the answer to the question, but the sagacious investigator will keep looking. The I Am Presence is awaiting just beyond the mind to reveal Itself as your Essential Nature.

The mind insists that you could not be Divine. It insists on separation and will often defend its position to the death. But the sage keeps looking and finds the true answer. That's why he's a sage.

Who Are You, Really?
10-1-07

Who are you, really?
Go inside for a moment
Find the ordinary everyday garden variety "you"
The "you" that looks out your eyes
That hears through your ears, that thinks

Can you feel that?
Can you feel yourself?

My friend, THAT is God
The ultimate perceiver
Yet you imagine that it is you

That thought
And that thought alone
Is what separates you
From God

Commentary: Your Holy Eyes

The mind is not the tool to find God. This trap has snared so many wonderful seekers: the assumption that God is another object for the mind to perceive. That never happens and will frustrate you to tears if you try. God is not an object and your mind is not the subject.

The mind is good for so many things that we reflexively use it when we begin the spiritual search. But the mind is not the tool to use to find God. Instead, use what is aware of the mind — Consciousness.

Your Holy Eyes
10-30-2000

Stop grabbing God
And throwing Her in a sack

God is not going to fit
In your big beautiful mind
Minds were not built to house God
They were built as a lens to perceive

God is not an object
Not something you "have"
Mind cannot grasp It
Or contain It

What you can do — is "Be It"
And let Her look through your holy eyes

Commentary: There is Only God

This is pure non-dual perspective.

The voice in the poem is not the ego speaking.
It is not the "I-thought" in the mind. It is not the
subject to a world full of objects.

This is Awareness speaking. This is the bridge
between the transcendent and the individualized,
deepening together day by day.

There is Only God

2-4-2000

Almighty indwelling God
My unending gratitude
For allowing me
To be part of this expanding play

I laugh
I cry

I say there is a "You" and an "I"
We laugh together at this little lie
There is only You
But not different than I

Commentary: The Truth

I had been doing the Saraswathi truth mantra for months when this poem emerged and I had fallen head over heels in love with the truth. The truth is so clean and pure and true. The mantra attunes you to the truth. It cultures the ability to hear the truth and speak the truth.

This poem burst forth one morning and wrote itself. The last line defines truth.

The Truth
8-5-07

The Truth is such a lover
She ruins you for anyone else
To fly is to have Her under your wings
There isn't enough muscle in your wing to fly without Her

With Her we surrender to "what is"
And we are given back our freedom

Freedom from what?
Freedom from the mind's tyranny
Over the heart

Truth is non-resistance to what is

Commentary: Listening

When I use the term "story", I am not talking about the wonderful world of mythology or narrative storytelling, which is a beautiful tradition. I use the term "story" to mean an uninvestigated belief.

Ideas need to be felt within the heart to determine their truth. This is discernment. The mind presents a thought, idea or belief to the heart and then asks, "Is this thought true?" The heart feels the truth or falsity of the thought and responds in its own silent language. If you accept an idea without this heart-mind discernment, then I suggest you are creating a "story" that you do not know to be true. Why would you do that? The answer can be found in the mind, as ego. Ego is the unobserved mind operating without the witnessing presence.

Listening traces the path of *embracing*, which is turning your full awareness to and opening to the energy. The information as to *why* a feeling is arising is embedded within the energy of the emotional. Open to the emotion; blend with it, listen and feel. It will reveal all its secrets to you if you listen.

The idea is presented that anger and frustration are indications that you haven't listened and you haven't communicated something. Instead of engaging the usual approach of suppressing or expressing your anger, the solution might be as simple as asking yourself, "What haven't I communicated?" That shifts you out of the anger into listening.

Listening
7-5-08

If you are angry or frustrated
It means you stopped listening
Whatever story the mind was selling — you bought it
You can listen or you can tell a story
But you can't do both at the same time
They're mutually exclusive

When you believe a thought
Without asking your heart if it is true
Then that thought becomes your belief
In a sense, your story

The problem with such stories
Is that you stop listening
You "buy" the thought without further investigation
THAT disconnects you from the truth

Thought is inherently disconnected
From Essence, from Source
You are its connection
If you go missing, it has no connection

CONTINUED >>

Your listening
Connects your thought
To the spiritual heart
The heart is what knows the way

If you abandon your listening
For a story
Don't come complaining
About your bad results

Open hearted listening is the royal road
The heart blends with the energy
Revealing the way to you
Providing the missing information your story is lacking

"That is what the 'crushing' is all about:

Your unwillingness

To let your Divine Nature

Run the show"

You Came Here To Get Your Wings pg 261

Commentary: The Nature of Life

You get what you focus on — whether you like it or not. Even in a world where love is always available to you, this law remains firmly rooted. There is contrast; there is still positivity and negativity and all sorts of madness. Your choice! By your attention, your choice is implemented.

The masters say, "Above all else, worship Love." If you choose not Love, the illusion comes calling. It brings you the lesson. Maya hurts!

This poem reveals a precious secret in the final three lines. Whatever movement you make towards Love, towards the Divine, towards God, will come back to you exponentially. Your every step will be multiplied over and over and given back to you. That is the promise from the immortals.

The Nature of Life
10-5-07

Even though the nature of life is Love
Illusion and agitation are always available to you

The immortals say, "Above all else, worship love"
But when you sacrifice love for illusion, you suffer
You lose your beautiful Self
In the reflections of the dream

Ask — simply ask!

Every step you take toward Her
She will take ten steps towards you

Commentary: The Surrender of Struggle

The issue of struggle versus effortlessness is the fork in the road. The path of struggle leads one way and the path of effortlessness leads another. It is where the ascent to self-recognition separates from the path of effort, control and dominance.

The path of effortlessness is the path of reconnecting with the transcendent Self that we are. Individuality opens to the transpersonal. We struggle because we deny that connection, and in our felt sense of separation, we push, we effort for what is already ours.

Why be a point, forcing its way through a field, when you are also the field?

The Surrender of Struggle
2-24-09

We are constantly in the embrace of the Mother
We are never alone. Our search to find God
Is the very effort that keeps Her at a distance
We deny that we are already in Her arms

Trying is a denial of what exists
It suggests that there is a lack within us

We came to this world to perceive our possibilities
For the sake of Consciousness finding Itself
Accept the gift that you are Divine
And always have been

There is no accomplishing this
There is no getting there
There is only realizing
That you already are there

The source of love — the Mother Herself

Commentary: Divine Qualities

In our culture we think of the human emotional range as moving from rage or shame on the low end all the way up to love, ecstasy or enlightenment on the high end.

The emotional range, however, naturally divides itself into two ranges, if you look at it from the perspective of what sources the emotion. Let me explain.

If a feeling is rooted in the ego, then it is an emotion. These would include all the negative feelings we are familiar with, as well as the positive ones such as happiness, which are based on things going our way.

But there is an altogether different range of feelings that is not ego-based, but Soul-based. This range includes qualities like love, patience, gratitude. These feelings are really not emotions, because they are not mind-generated. They are more appropriately called divine qualities, because they exude from the Soul or Divine Nature inherent in everyone.

The poem *Divine Qualities* introduces this perspective.

Divine Qualities
7-9-2000

Mind and its personality
Don't reach into majesty
If you want the divine qualities
Then open to the Soul

Because only there
Do the high frequency qualities flow
Only there
Is love the way it is

The Soul is love
Is kindness, is presence itself
The mind just makes up stories
 About these things

Commentary: You are the Pilot

The unobserved mind has a bad reputation. When there is no operator present to inform it, the mind operates on autopilot. The poem carries this theme forward. It is a teaching poem in that it ties together many different elements to present an empowering perspective.

It presents the idea that it is YOU who bring order to the mind through being present as the witnessing consciousness. If you are lost in thought, then you are asleep at the wheel.

NOW would be a good time to wake up. You wake up by returning to the here and now moment with your witnessing consciousness.

The poem describes what the mind is and how to discriminate using the heart and mind together. It suggests a possible cause for how we all got started in the dominating and controlling business. It describes the creation field and finishes by putting you squarely in the driver's seat of free will.

You Are The Pilot
7-5-08

Mind is an instrument of perception for the
Witnessing consciousness, for the perceiver
It's a tool of perception that relies on the operator
To order it, to command it

The airplane is the pilot's instrument
It completely relies on the pilot
Just so, mind relies on you
To connect it to Essence, to Truth

By itself, mind does not know Essence
It can't even recognize consciousness

If the pilot falls asleep at the wheel
The plane will soon destroy itself
It's the same with human beings
It just takes longer

Perceivers who get lost in thought
Go to sleep
The mind loses its operator
It loses its connection to the Truth, to reality

CONTINUED >>

With no one to connect it with the Truth
The mind wanders off into separation and craziness
That's not the plane's fault
That's pilot error !

YOU are the commanding element
The mind relies on you to inform it
If the witnessing presence has not yet awakened in you
Where is it?

Please — wake up
YOU are the witnessing presence
You are the perceiver
You are the pilot

The heart is what orders a human being
It is our connection to the Truth
It is where we "feel"
Our connection to Source

That Essence "orders" us
It puts us in right order
We then order the mind and life turns sweet

So, dear friend
Don't fall asleep at the wheel

Listen to your Heart
What is it whispering in your ear?

If you can't hear your heart, then ask
Each thought, each emotion: "Is this thought true?"
Let your heart read the thought and tell you if it's true
You can feel whether something is positive or negative

Once you have awakened from the mind trance
You take your rightful place at the helm
You become a deliberate creator, informed by Essence
An expression of the divine image of God

"Oh yes," you say
"I want to control the mind
But I want to control the world, too
I want others to do what I want them to do"

Oh sweetie, the world is so weary of that
So achingly weary !

Why do you want to control others?
Have you ever considered that?

CONTINUED >>

You probably noticed that when
Things went your way — you felt better!
So you started forcing others to do things your way
So you could feel better

And then things got out of hand
One thing led to another
And here you are

That's all well and good if you want to force your way
Through creation but the shadows follow you

All thought is creative
It draws unto itself
Circumstances that match its nature
Whether you like it or not

Which condemns you
To what you focus upon
A negative focus begets negative results
A positive focus generates positive results

There is no getting around it
It's just the physics of this place
It's designed to crush you
As long as you focus negatively

That's the brilliance of letting the heart order your life
You become free of this negativity
The heart is your guidance system
It feels the way — it tells you the truth

That is free will — that is the choice you really have
To focus on what uplifts you
Or focus on what suppresses you
Your choice

Commentary: Bitter Root

This poem asks the question, "Why do you focus negatively?" In duality, all possibilities exist, both positive and negative, light and dark. Just because something exists, doesn't mean you should focus on it.

The dinner buffet table is an ideal metaphor here. The buffet is loaded with food, more than you could ever eat. Some of it you like and some of it you don't. You put on your plate what you like eating and leave the rest for others. If it's on the buffet table, someone probably likes it, even if you don't. That is exactly the condition we live in.

If you don't want something, don't focus on it.

Bitter Root

9-10-07

Why chew on a bitter root
When there is sooooo much magnificence?
It's all true
But why eat it when the Feast is here?

The grapes of gratitude
The sweet melon of appreciation
The luscious peach of loving

Why fill up on weeds
When the nourishing grains are here?

Your focus is your meal

Nourish yourself, sweet angel
Nourish your Self

Commentary: Tjehuthi

Tjehuthi is the Egyptian name for a magnificent master of the Solar Line who was physically embodied for 16,000 years. He was the one who brought the sacred knowledge from the crumbling Atlantis and reseeded it into the Nile River region which would later become Egypt. The Greeks called him Thoth.

I had a haunting affinity with Tjehuthi from the moment I heard his name.

In the spring of 2008, I was helping initiate two of my friends into the Sambodha knowledge. We met in Dr Rosie's yurt on the third day of the training to practice the *Adipavana* together. In the middle of the meditation, Tjehuthi entered the room as an immense field of presence above us. I was speechless as a deep reverence welled up in me. Warm hot tears of love and devotion flowed down my face.

He wordlessly said that the four of us had been together in the temples of Egypt during the fall of consciousness. The energy had fallen so low during those times that the sacred knowledge had been withdrawn. The energy had now risen sufficiently so that we were coming back together to continue the work. I was in awe and reverence as I sat weeping at the magnificent immensity of the presence. Then, as quickly as he arrived, he was gone.

Thousands of years ago, Tjehuthi had withdrawn the sacred knowledge as the world descended into the dark yuga. The samyamas were too powerful to be allowed in the hands of the ignorant and greedy.

The forty books of Tjehuthi were hidden in the secret rooms at the Library of Alexandria until it was sacked and burned. Even the Book of Maat was withdrawn. These precious teachings would stay protected in other dimensions until the time for their return. That time is now.

I wrote the Tjehuthi poem from this awe and reverence. The question lingered: "Who are you, Tjehuthi? What order of Being must you be that you so completely overwhelm me?" It is as if Archangel Michael, in all his glory, appeared in front of me, reached into my chest and opened my heart. My knees would buckle as I caved into this immense swelling devotion. Even now I feel a profound affinity and can be moved to tears when his name is spoken.

Tjehuthi
4-30-08

You come to me — my chest explodes
You enter my heart — my Soul falls to its knees
One breath of you — overwhelms me
Opens the dimensional door
Expands me beyond speech

Tjehuthi, Tjehuthi, Tjehuthi: who are you?
Some magnificent Being
My Soul had the good fortune
To meet, to know — perhaps, to love?

Just knowing your name excites something so deep
As if the Soul built a bridge from heaven and you
Walked right across it — into my body
Your Presence, a river flowing through me

Words fail me, all thoughts disappear
My heart breaks loose from its moorings
The Soul falls to its knees in reverence
Oh, Tjehuthi, lord of these hot tears

Make your home in my heart

Undefended
8-24-07

Beloved Self
To You, I am undefended
If You want to cry
Please, let me be Your eyes

If You want to praise
Let me be Your mouth
If You want to caress
Let me be Your hand

Together, ego and Soul
Walk hand in hand — not two really

Commentary: Weird Failures

Before you butt heads with the universe, it's good to understand what you're up against — but that almost never happens. We come in swinging, or crushed, or angry. No one tells us what is really going on here.

The purpose of life is to vessel the Transcendent, not to fulfill the dream that your culture is selling you. The "perfect" life is not going to do it. It's empty. Check it out for yourself; talk with someone who has accomplished "perfect", someone who has the perfect job or the perfect marriage, or the perfect anything. The honest ones will tell you it's not fulfilling. It's not fulfilling because it's a concept and never had a basis in your deeper reality.

Yes, the money is nice and the relationship is nice, but it is not fulfilling unless it's authentic. You have to look deeper than the cultural dream. You have to look into what is true for YOU.

What this poem suggests is that if you are playing the game of life from the external side of things, forcing, efforting, and struggling, then you have not gone deep enough to find your authentic purpose for being. If you are just working it from the surface, then life will thwart you to tears.

Weird Failures
6-23-2000

You are trying to make it in the world
You struggle and strive
You are sure that with enough effort
You can make it

I'm sorry to be the one to tell you, sweetheart
But this place is not designed to work!!!
It is designed to crush you
So that you turn inside

Creation is a physical projection
Of what is inside your mind
If you work it solely from the outside
The weird failures never end

Commentary: The Father Brought Silence

When the primordial Oneness separated Itself to form duality, the first split was into the Father and the Mother. The Father is consciousness and will. The Mother is power and energy. The Mother is the birthing power that brings reality into existence. The Father is the consciousness that enlivens and sustains the worlds.

The love that these two have for each other creates everything in existence: all the dimensions, all the universes, everything seen and unseen.

The Mother is the love. So when I talk of Her I am talking about God as love. When I talk about Him, I am referring to God as awareness, will, wisdom.

When the Mother who is love touches you, there is only melting and gratitude.

The Father Brought Silence
4-28-08

The Father brought silence
A vast oceanic stillness
In which Awareness
Is aware of Itself

But the Mother . . .
The Mother brought Love
Her Nature is Sweetness Itself

Even as this pen
Makes its way across the page
She pours Herself over me
And I am drunk

When She opens to you
When She opens to you
Your life will never be the same

Commentary: Allowing

This poem is another attempt to express the pure brilliance of allowing. To understand why allowing is so brilliant, you must appreciate the underlying physics of our world. Our universe is a field of magnetism. I call it a Creation Field, because whatever you place your attention upon is drawn to you.

What that means is, there is no NO in the universe, there is only YES. If you put your attention on something, you are saying yes to it. It is your command to the universe to give you more of it.

Are you beginning to see the brilliance? The only way to say NO to anything is to remove your attention from it and allow it to be. To push against something, you must put your attention on it, which is the request to the universe to give you more of it. It is the same with fighting; you are requesting more of what you really don't want.

Successful people understand not to focus on the problem, but on the solution. The Bible says this in its own way: "Resist not evil." By allowing, you give the shadow permission to exist in duality. Allowing is how you manage your focus. Anything else binds you.

Allowing
5-30-2008

What you cannot allow — owns you
It is the life-shaping fear that haunts
Allowing releases you
Resisting binds you

Can you allow your own failure?
Your own death?
Until you can allow all possibilities
The mind binds you in its cage

Allowing is freedom
Freedom to create
Freedom to express
Freedom to love

What you are free of
Is the mind's constant distortion
Of your beautiful sweet Nature

Sonjan's Story and the Solar Lineage

The story goes back to meeting Babaji in 1969.
I was in flight training in Pensacola when the Navy
determined it had too many pilots. Their solution
was to empty out the training program. I left the
Navy and headed home, still subject to military
service. The Army was actively drafting for Vietnam
and my draft-lottery number turned out to be 24,
meaning, I was guaranteed to be drafted.

A vision led me to read The Autobiography of a
Yogi. In it Babaji vows, "Anyone who sincerely
prays in my name will have their prayer answered."
I opened the book to Babaji's picture, put it under
my pillow and prayed night after night: "I don't
want to go to war. I want to find God. If you keep
me out of this war, I will sincerely seek for God."
And that is exactly what happened.

Within three weeks, a draft notice arrived; I was
classified "1Y", physically unfit for service. I didn't
ask how one of the Navy's own could be classified
"unfit". Babaji had simply answered my prayer.
I did not go to war. I began kriya meditation
with Self Realization Fellowship using Babaji's
techniques passed down through Yogananda. That
was my first encounter with the Solar Lineage.

In 1992 Ramana Maharshi found me through the
returning luminaries from Papaji's satsang hall. I
was on fire with inquiry and sat with everyone who

was teaching. I studied with Bartholomew from '92 to '96; it was pure Ramana Maharshi.

In June of '97 something happened, an epiphany. I called it a foreground/background shift. The identity that had been running in the foreground disappeared into the background and what had been running silently in the background came forward as Silence. Awareness had recognized Itself.

I came to understand this as the core recognition underlying the first realization. A mild bliss now flowed through me most of the time.

I began working with Gangaji who skillfully put language to what was essentially unspeakable. Her talent never ceased to amaze me. But as the years passed, I started to feel that there was more to spiritual life than silence, more to it than dissolving in Essential Nature. From deep within the silence emerged the impulse, "Now that you are awake, WHAT IS POSSIBLE?"

Inquiry had taken me as far as it could. It had yielded its fruit. As delicious as silence was, there was more. The call became so loud that I actually began to feel stuck in silence. I know that sounds crazy, but the Mother was whispering in my ear, saying that there was more to life than silence. I was being called back into life. This was Vishnu's call. I was being asked to pick up the power of creation and actualize.

I saw that the Shiva model, the 'consciousness only' model of dissolution in one's Essential Nature, was a flawed ideal. In reality, we do NOT lose our individuality; we gain our universality. The drop does not dissolve in the Ocean; the Ocean enters the drop.

The 'no self' approach is not a life-oriented path and does not lead to fulfillment. Dissolution is not the goal and neither is silence. Consciousness is only half the adventure. It is the combination of both consciousness *and* energy that creates Life; both need embracing. The path is expression, not dissolution. Joy, Love and Eternal Life are the principles seeking expression.

The satsang circuit was full of luminous teachers, but everyone was speaking of silence, dissolution, 'no-self'. I began working with my friend Aaravindha.

He was the voice of Vishnu and the Mother. And he was about to set off on the journey of a lifetime. He had been invited to the Valley of the Masters.

After his trek to the Himalayas, he shared his experiences with the Sambodha community. He told us the story of his trek and his time with the masters of the Solar Lineage (Arka Vamsha). He was radiant with their power and the heart connection was huge. I silently reached out to these masters and said "I am ready" and they reached across time and connected with me.

Aaravindha was the only teacher I knew who was addressing the unfulfilling aspect of silence and I wanted to devour his teaching. He was speaking with authority about the deepest levels of consciousness. He wasn't passing on lineage curriculum. He was looking directly into Divine Mind. He was staring into eternity.

I wanted to know if his teachings were congruent with the understanding that had matured within me. I went to Europe and entered the teacher training courses where the core knowledge is taught. Over the course of a year, I discovered that he indeed understood everything I knew; yet the depth of his understanding just kept going.

Every master I knew, understood that self-recognition was not the end, but the beginning. All awakening leads to further deepening. This was my deepening.

It is out of this shift from the dissolution-oriented 'consciousness only' Shiva school to the Life-oriented 'consciousness *and* energy' Vishnu school that these poems came into existence.

Silence is essential, but instead of dissolving in silence and stillness, one listens to what is moving through silence; one listens for the Divine Intention that wants to enter life and answer the need in the world.

It is the Mother's Voice speaking to you, and the Mother wants paradise, not dissolution.

Commentary: Oracle

As I work with Aaravindha, I gain an ever-deeper appreciation for his ability. He is a rishi, a seer. Until you spend time around someone with this skill, it's hard to imagine the scope of the gift. He has direct access into Divine Mind.

I could see that we shared the same passion for the sacred, for wisdom and divine knowledge. I could see what inspires him. It is the same thing that inspires me.

The more personal time I spend with him, the more and more amazed I become at his *saumedhika* sight. This is the ancient Sanskrit name for this oracular ability. This was an ability of immense proportion.

You could do anything in the world with such a gift, but he has dedicated his life to world service, to sharing his gift with the world. What a blessing and we are the beneficiaries.

This poem springs from my awe and appreciation for the enormity of his gift and his willingness to share it.

Oracle
10-16-07

We share the same passion for God
And love, and True Self Knowledge
I can see what lights you up
I see what lifts you into the Solar Winds

What a gift — what a phenomenal gift
Saumedhika sight !
To see into the vault of time
An open door into Divine Mind

I had no idea how sweet Her gifts could be
You must be very loved to come out of the oven
So blessed — I know, all skills need honing and, yes,
The gifted are persecuted — the flock resents genius

And yet the hero comes from the village
Captures the sacred and brings it back home
You are that hero, Aaravindha
You came back from the valley full of light

Now — here we all are — a luminous blessing

Commentary: There is no How

I use my trusted metaphor in this poem, the point and the field, to answer the mind's eternal question — 'How?' The mind in denial of its Source does feel separate and disconnected. It's true. It eternally whines: "How do I do this and how do I do that?" Well, silly, if you didn't separate yourself in the first place, you wouldn't have to whine, you could just open and get the answer.

The answer appears mysteriously when we open. It was there all along, but couldn't be seen until we opened. Any of the 'how's' will work, once your heart is open and asking.

When this poem came through, there was so much energy moving. The last stanza broke the dam, and the floodgate opened.

There is no How
9-5-07

You can be luminous
You can be full of light
Open yourself, just OPEN

Let the local address yield to the Non-Local
Let the "point" relax into the Field
How ?   There is no how ! ! !
Just open

And — there are a thousand hows:
Meditation
Prayer
Mantra
Whirling

Any way will work
For the Heart
On its knees
Asking

Commentary: The Subject

This poem continues the investigation that began in *Who Are You, Really?* It's a theme that repeats throughout the book. It is the issue of identity, so pivotal to waking up from the trance of mind.

I wanted to bring the idea of the lower self, as ego, and the higher Self, as your Divine Nature, out of the clouds of abstraction and make it real. What are we really talking about here? You often hear people say in conversation "my ego", to which I usually respond, "Then who are you?" The question is usually met with a stunned silence.

As a culture, we have no training in who we are. There is no moment of exploration of what we mean when we say "I". We are rushed by that sacred opportunity into function and identity: "Hurry up, Billy, you'll miss the school bus." Function is wonderful, but by itself, it breeds a culture that knows only what they are, and not who they are.

So I ask the question, "Who are you?" What experience are you referring to when you say 'I'?" I know it seems absurd even to ask such a question from the perspective of a function-oriented world. But in a moment of quiet investigation, enter your inner landscape and observe your operating system. If you are like most of us, you will find the mind is operating as if it were the subject, the center, the king pin, to a world of objects.

That assumed subject is the ego. Ego is a mind-generated function. It's the uninvestigated, unobserved you in the mind. But that is not the real you.

That "you" is not self-aware. Just check and see. There is something else that is aware of it, illuminating it; that something else is the real you. It's the shine of consciousness, your True Nature, the I Am Presence that is the ultimate perceiver.

As long as the mind is running unobserved the real you is not present. In the poems I call this the unobserved mind or the disconnected mind and its nature is self-serving and tyrannical. It sees itself as separate and fights to survive. It's a mechanism.

Awareness is invisible to mind. The mind cannot see it, hear it, taste it or touch it. The mind cannot see consciousness. The mind senses it, senses the presence of Being, but has no mechanism to perceive it, similar to the eye not being able to see itself. So the mind makes a clone of consciousness. It makes Being into something it can relate to. It makes it into a thought, the "I" thought.

That means that awareness must become aware of itself, and that is exactly what waking up is. Once you begin to observe the goings on of the mind with witnessing consciousness, then the journey home accelerates.

The Subject

6-2-06

How do you sleep?
You pull the covers of thought
Over your beautiful face
And dream the "I"

The mind is a sea of thought
In which you have lost your way
You dream of separation
Assuming yourself to be the subject

But the "I" in the mind is not the real "I"
It is not the subject at all
Something larger is aware of it

How else could you be seduced out of Eternal Being?
You were enticed with the promise
Of being separate from everyone else
And you took the bait

Now, here you are, deep in the illusion
Of being a somebody going somewhere

Yet, you are not happy
You are no longer enjoying your journey
You have become a whining nuisance
Telling stories about how God did it to you

You drunk angel
You're so intoxicated with individuality
That you have forgotten who you are

Have you heard of Love?
Have you heard of Oneness?
Have you heard the Saints whispering in the corner
About enlightenment?

Yes, you can be free!
You can be Love
You can have it all
But not if you are there

Not as long as you insist
On being the "local address"
Not as long as you insist
On being "the subject" to a world full of objects

CONTINUED >>

This is the trance that binds you
There is something larger going on
A vast field of awareness
Which you have simply overlooked

Ask yourself this:
"What is aware of this subject
I assume myself to be?"

The dream is in the mind
You stop the dream by stopping the mind
There is a pause after every thought
Explore that pause

By stopping thought
You see directly what remains
In the stillness
You meet your Self

How long does it take?
How long does it take
To wake up from a dream?

"The seed tones in the divine language

become the vibration you follow

through the mind, through silence

and beyond the mind

into the Truth Expanse"

Commentary on Red Eyes, pg 247

Spirit and Soul

In this book, I have used the terms Soul and Spirit interchangeably. For the purposes of poetry, I have used them synonymously. When I say Soul, it is same as saying Spirit.

However, they are not identical. Spirit, is the eternal consciousness, the I Am presence animating all life. God is Spirit and Spirit is God. It is the Divine eternal reality. It is what IS before creation occurred and shall BE after creation passes away. Spirit is what is.

Soul is a field of life force that Spirit informs, impresses, or you could say — inhabits. Soul allows Spirit to have an individual perspective, to work with mind as an instrument of perception, and enter lower dimensional realms with function and memory.

The Soul is a vehicle for the Spirit as the physical body is a vehicle for the Soul. It's a step-down transformer that allows Spirit to enter this world.

Dharma
10-17-08

What you have to decide
Is whether the mind can make you happy

Do you yield to Spirit, letting the Divine
Order your life, or do you choose mind as your
Guiding principle?

Weigh this carefully
The pursuit of happiness has a Dark side
The disconnected mind serves only itself

There is another way, traveler
In "dharma" the mind surrenders to Spirit
And listens for divine intention

Surrendering the mind — opens the Heart
Returns authenticity, restores innocence
Instead of the mind trying to achieve what it can
Never achieve, the open heart naturally radiates sweetness

The choice is eternally yours

Commentary: The Mad Adventure

Life in the forge is hot. You are heated, then hammered over and over. Life is shaping you through pain. It goes on until you are so tired of it that you become willing to change. Until then, you get hammered.

This poem speaks about it as an adventure, a mad adventure in the illusion of separation. As soon as you leave love for the condition of the illusion, you are in free fall. What looked so wonderfully alluring turned out to be a disaster.

If you're in this condition, you are probably angry, mad that things didn't go your way. But if you trace the roots of your choices, you can see where you have chosen judgment over love, anger over joy, and war over peace. It was your choices that led you downward.

The way out of the forge is not a pursuit nor a search, but a recognition that you were not separate in the first place, that there is only One being here and you are a part of that One being, and so is everybody and everything else. This realization puts you back in right order, where you can learn through joy.

The Mad Adventure
4-14-06

Your altar broke
The moment you pushed aside
Her gifts of Love and joy
To make room for separation

Yet your gift has lead to sadness
You rail at your brother
You get mad at yourself
Tell me "What sane mind attacks itself?"

This adventure of separation has gone awry
You gave away compassion, for what — judgment?
You gave away your peace — for war
Now you've lost your joy, and you're angry

What started out with such enthusiasm
Has somehow gone terribly wrong
The road Home, is really no road at all
The way Home, is realizing you already are Home

The illusion is all in the mind

Commentary: Divine Lovers

It has been said that gratitude and love are so close vibrationally that one can hardly tell them apart.

But God and love are even closer, like lovers. Even closer than lovers, like water and wetness. No, even closer than that, but how do you say it?

Here is how I say it: To let love have you is to let God have you.

Take the leash off.

Divine Lovers
10-11-07

Love, Wisdom, Beauty, Truth and Freedom
All the divine qualities are sacred

But God and Love
Have something going on ! ! !
They are such lovers
You can't tell them apart

To separate them — unthinkable!
Worse than wrestling wetness from water

All attempts to control Love
Are attempts to control God

Take the leash off and let Her run
Her footsteps just might save you

Commentary: Beauty and the Heart

Beauty is the expression of Truth. To love beauty is to love the Truth in form. Appreciation of beauty is the appreciation of Truth in form.

If true beauty doesn't just overwhelm us, then the heart needs to open wider, because it doesn't yet appreciate the depth of the Truth.

In this poem, knees are a metaphor for having found sincerity and humility.

Beauty and the Heart
9-3-07

Weeping, cracking open
Falling to our knees
That is the Heart's response
To beauty

If we are not overwhelmed by beauty
It's a sign that we need more time in the oven
The knees have not been made ready
For what the Heart will soon bring

Commentary: Wanting to Know

It is not your brother's job to prove anything to you. It is our job to open and listen for our self. Go ahead, stay in your mind with your arms and legs crossed. In time suffering will soften you and you will return to opening. Until then, you're in the grinder. I wish you good luck.

No one can do it for you or prove it to you. It's not anyone else's job. It's your job and your journey.

This poem started as a result of a conversation with a friend who was saying that when she was teaching and initiating in the larger cities, she was experiencing people with the "prove it to me" attitude. We started talking about how the teaching process works, what happens when a true teacher meets a true student.

We are accustomed to teachers who box up their truth and want to sell us their box. If we're interested, we say: "Prove that your box is better than mine and perhaps I will become your follower." But that is not a true teacher; that is a preacher. He wants to tell you the way it is, rather than to invite you into your self.

The teacher's job is to invite you into your own experience. It is the student's receptivity, sincerity, and openness that summon the answer from within. Being receptive means to open your heart and listen. If the student hasn't lifted into real receptivity within him or herself, there is very little anyone can do.

Wanting to Know

5-3-08

Wanting to know
That is how the adventure begins

From there, you have a choice
Go into the mind and demand proof, or
Go into your heart and listen

Your choice !

It is your own Self that you will come to know
It is your Self that your Soul will unwrap for you

Become receptive to yourself
What do you feel?
Do you feel your heart?
Can you feel your existence?

That is where your answers are going to show up
In your heart
The information you seek
Is imbedded within that energy

CONTINUED >>

Stay authentic
What is your heart telling you?
Listen, feel . . .
What does the silent language tell you?

Now, discriminate with that brilliant mind
Read the energy, taste it, savor it
Swirl it around within your heart
You can tell what feels good and what feels bad

What is your own heart saying to you?
Let the questions bubble up
 It is the authentic question arising
That summons the answer

Learn the language of your Heart
Your Soul always is speaking to you
But you must open and listen
You will need this skill on your journey

A good teacher invites you
Into your own experience
Your Soul then unfolds Its wisdom
To a waiting ear

A bad teacher — well, a bad teacher offers you
A closed teaching
And demands belief, not listening
They preach, as if only they knew
They assert, as if only they were right

Beloved pilgrim of God
The True Teacher lives within you
It is the Self which resides as your true Heart
Listen to That!

Commentary: The Purpose of Life

The purpose of life is to embody the Divine. You are here on Earth to bring the Transcendent Self that you are into physical reality and allow It to shine. That Shine will transform you and this world into paradise. That's what you came here to do — no matter what.

It's your job to find out who you are and actualize it. Are you a man or woman, a success, a failure, a doctor or a carpenter? All these are identity traps that offer you a distraction from your discovery. They may be "what" you are for a moment, but never 'who' you are. Who you are is the transcendent glory that sources this world.

It's a tall order to step into a physical body full of appetites and needs, into a mind that doesn't know who you are, into a duality packed full of contrast and a culture that's externally oriented — but that is what you came to do.

Our vulnerability is that we fall into separation and forget who we are. We believe the appearance. When you discover yourself as Divine Nature, the identities fall away and you become yourself. Your mind becomes a servant and your body, an instrument of expression. The divine qualities flow naturally as an expression of your nature. Your heart opens and love pours forth in compassion for the staggering difficulty of the journey and you become a light unto the world.

The Purpose of Life
5-10-09

You have come here to embody the Transcendent
To realize and actualize your Divine Essence

But in our way stands the mind with its ego
And a freshly tied blindfold
The world seduces us, all of us
We forget who we are as we tumble into the senses

My God, the crushing we endure
Before the Lights come back on

The way Home is the way to our Self
We discover Love
We find the Truth
We release our dysfunctions in the divine forge

Home is here — now — your Divine Nature
Your Transcendent Self
The luminous Light
Shining through your eyes

Meditation and Brain States

In talking with meditators, the language we hear goes something like this — silence, stillness, altered states (aka samadhi or satori) and some term like "monkey mind " to refer to obsessive thinking. In science we hear a different language. Scientists speak of brain states as wave frequencies, such as beta, alpha, theta and delta.

Beta is between 13 and 40 brainwave cycles per second. Alpha is between 7 and 12 cycles; theta between 4-7 cycles and delta is below 4 cycles. Beta is considered normal waking consciousness and delta is considered sleep.

My sense of it is this: beta is what meditators call monkey mind. Thoughts are nearly continuous. Attention is constantly absorbed in thought and emotion. There is very little free attention here.

The next state down is alpha. Alpha is the beginning of silence. Thoughts have subsided and there is now free awareness between thought. This is the state of mindfulness that spiritual traditions culture; being in the here-and-now-moment, aware, with no thought, restful alertness. However, thoughts do still occur here, but at a much-reduced rate.

Theta is yet a deeper state, around seven cycles. This is what I call stillness. In this state, thoughts cease to arise. It feels like fresh fallen snow, pristine stillness. Awareness is free to enjoy its own nature without thought. What started in alpha as silence has now deepened into stillness as all thought ceases. This is Patanjali's definition of meditation (dhyana) in the Yoga Sutras, the seventh stage of Yoga.

People who have never experienced a cessation of thought may argue that such a condition does not exist. I was attacked once in an Actualization seminar for reporting on my meditation experience. A beautiful young woman vehemently argued that what I described was impossible. However, this is precisely where deep rejuvenating peace is experienced — the peace that passeth understanding.

Beyond 'no thought', the game deepens. Meditators generally consider silence and stillness the end of the journey. You have arrived. Brain scientists say that less than four cycles per second you enter Delta and you are asleep.

I say no, no, no. This is just where the process gets interesting. Beyond silence (alpha) and stillness (theta) there is a field. I call it the Truth Expanse. But the brain waves are so slow, that it takes training to stay conscious in this realm of long , slow, undulating brain waves. This is a state highly valued by yogis. The body is essentially immobile. The senses are withdrawn. This is the doorway to altered states of consciousness, the portal to other dimensions. Patanjali's Yoga Sutras call these states samadhi, the eighth and culminating stage of Raja Yoga.

The reason we don't hear of samadhi states or other dimensions in our culture is because so few people stay conscious at this level of brain wave activity. This takes meditation training and lots of it. Most of us are so habituated to thinking that these realms are inaccessible other than through trauma or medical emergency. But they are there nonetheless, for those traveling the less traveled road.

Keep an Eye on It

3-25-06

The disconnected mind is such a tyrant
A sly jailer of the offspring of God
Left on its own
It imprisons us in thought

Only the mind that listens to the Friend
Can be trusted
Only the mind that serves the Heart
Can be followed

Even then — I keep an eye on it!

Commentary: Sarvamahat

The Sarvamahat is a meditation. It empowers
three aspects. It uses the Truth Vidya Mantra
to empower the ability to hear the truth purely.
Secondly, it cultures the power of shakti to
empower the truth. Thirdly, it stabilizes you on
the surface of that expanse in pure perception.

The meditation is given to the teachers in the
Sambodha tradition in their third year of work.
As the mantra is repeated quietly in the mind, it
softens until it arises out of the silence of presence,
an impulse. The frequency of the unspoken tones
moves into the truth expanse. The mind learns
to adjust to the expansiveness as it leaves all
references behind.

The Sarvamahat poem is an attempt to express
the inexpressible. As perception gets more and
more expanded, the landscape changes. You move
beyond the mind into pure perception, but how do
you get beyond your mind, when that is where all
your references are? The poem asks the question:
Can you stay awake when there is no "you" there?

This is where you park your mind and travel
onward by foot. You can't make this ascent by
staying within your mind. As Hafiz puts it, "If you
think that the Truth can be known from words —

somebody should start laughing; somebody should start wildly laughing."

The Sarvamahat meditation moves you beyond the mind. The poem is an attempt to transmit the feeling of the experience because it is so difficult to talk about in a linear way.

Sarvamahat
11-13-08

No reference
No subject-object
Nothing for the mind to recognize

Conscious mind loses interest, falls asleep
If you are identified within the mind
Then when mind goes to sleep — you go to sleep

But, for those of you traveling on
You will notice your Natural State
The boundless, objectless presence
That you are

Self-recognition is essential
Because until the Self recognizes Itself
How will you pass beyond the mind?

What reference would you use?
What will you be aware of?
How will you stay conscious
When everything you recognize fades into silence?

Can you stay awake
When your identity fades from view
And there is no "you" there?

There is another Self, which is always present
It is what is aware of your mind, your thoughts
It is what's aware of the "you"
That you assume yourself to be

This is the You that is calling
Can you hear your Self calling?
It is calling you Home
To Itself, to your Self

But self-recognition does not
Happen to you
It does not happen to the you
That you think you are

It is the larger You
Becoming aware of Itself

Commentary: I Have No Feet But Yours

Aligning with the Divine is good, but realizing the Divine as your own nature, is deeper. In poems like *I Have No Feet But Yours* and *The Pitcher Has Broken*, you can feel the intimacy. You can feel the separation slipping away.

I Have No Feet But Yours says that when God comes to earth, He comes as you and me. The Divine expresses as us!!! What an insight. It makes you fall to your knees in gratitude. We are the expression of the Divine.

When the heart opens to receive its Divine Nature, love floods through, the mouth becomes inspired and the heart overflows with gratitude.

I Have No Feet But Yours
4-30-2000

I would fall at Your feet
In gratitude, in weeping joy
But You say:
"Sweetheart, I have no feet but yours."

I fell to my knees
That God could be this close
This beautiful
This intimate

Now the grain sack has opened
And is spilling out
Those who long for the Friend
Are drawn to the nourishment

When the heart is torn open
Love can say what can't be said
She can lift Her light-filled cup
To your beautiful parched lips

Commentary: Divine Acorn

The *Divine Acorn* poem says, you can stop 'trying so hard'. Release the struggle; your destiny is assured. You are the prodigal son. You can return Home when you choose. Your great good fortune is this: You are what is eternal.

The poem presents the idea that creation is duality, where every topic is really two topics: the abundance and the absence of every item. There is health and sickness, wealth and poverty, hot and cold, up and down.

The exploration of the "injustices and suffering" is our outrage at the shadow, our refusal to allow duality, our insistence that things go our way, our resistance to the truth. It is where we push against what we don't want and can't accept. It is where we put on our plate what we really don't want — and then howl at the injustice of it.

The world has trained us to seek our power through effort, but your real power will come through listening.

Divine Acorn
7-17-08

Oh sweetheart, you are a divine acorn
The pride of your Father
The joy of your Mother

An acorn, a precious seed
Destined to grow into your Divine Nature
A sacred eternal presence

If you look for the Truth
You will find the Self
Why wander the deserts of your mind
When your destiny is assured?

You are what IS, my dear, eternal I Am-ness
Dancing your way through the kingdom

Here in creation
There's no shortage of contrast to explore
Every issue is two issues
Knock yourself out ! ! !

CONTINUED >>

But when you are through, when you are done
With the edges and the borders
The injustices and the suffering

Know that your destiny is secure
You are the prodigal son
The acorn can only become the oak

There is only One Home to return to
The Home that you once left
Your Father welcomes you
Your Mother rejoices at your return

Explore to your heart's content!
Your family is right beside you

The acorn can rail at its fate
Weep that it is not a mango
Sleep away lifetimes in ignorance
But its fate is sealed — it can only become what it is

You are that seed
You will become that tree
Your destiny has already happened
The only mystery — is when you come Home

Commentary: Getting There

This poem arose out of a compassion for all of us beginning the spiritual path. There are so many teachings and approaches that it's bewildering.

We begin the search by assuming the position of separation, then marching toward the goal of union with God.

But the 'getting there' approaches are just more of the same. They assume your separation to be true. Instead of revealing the lie, they make it the cornerstone of their path. They put you into a search, into a pursuit of the Divine. What you are looking for is your own Self. You are looking for "who is looking".

Belief systems are notorious for trapping us, so are religions and teachers. I make the admonition — don't be led astray; find someone who knows, who really knows.

This is Sonjan's conundrum: you can't get there by effort, and you can't get there without effort.

In the early stages there is effort: establishing a daily practice, discovering mindfulness, improving diet, engaging inquiry, doing 'the work'. If you don't put in that effort, then you won't develop the foundation skills needed to support the deeper work.

But as you deepen and begin discovering who you are, effort gives way to an ease-of-being. Effortlessness becomes your signature as you allow your Divine Essence to order your life. You no longer resist the divine intention flowing through you. You recognize it as your own intelligence.

Getting There
3-30-06

When you begin the journey
Enlightenment is a mountain far off in the distance

You can't get there by effort
And you can't get there without effort

Belief systems trap you
Religions obscure
Teachers are human
Find someone who knows

Pilgrim, I can tell you this
There is no 'getting there'
The way you get there
Is by realizing you are already there

Commentary: Holy One Dragged Me Here

I grew up in the suburbs of Southern California and I had all the *vrittis** to prove it. I had lived in San Diego, Santa Barbara and San Francisco. I had become a real estate broker. I loved wine, women and song — and success. But then I underwent a complete financial disaster in the real estate market and lost everything.

I was having an early mid-life crisis in which I realized that I had leaned my ladder against the wrong wall. I began looking for a new way of life. Not the fast life of the cities, real estate, and go-go business; that was too attractive, too alluring. I drove north feeling my way up the coast. I was looking for a spot that felt good: Mendocino, Ashland, Portland. I stopped when I found Orcas Island, a sleepy rural island with remarkable beauty and a mystical energy that had drawn healers and mystics for centuries. I was home.

The poem *The Holy One Dragged Me Here* expresses the revelation that matured over the years. I had been saved. The country had saved me from myself. I had been so attracted to the good life, that had I stayed in the city, I would have squandered another lifetime. I was rescued from my own tendencies. What a blessing.

The Holy One Dragged Me Here
5-10-2000

The Holy One
Dragged me out of the fast lane
Put me here
Far from the distractions of excess

Inner work is what She had in mind
And She did a good job — now the miracle begins

Giving away what can't be learned
Giving away what can't be taught

*Vrittis are mental ideas or concepts which have become habit
patterns. They act like a whirlpool, a rabbit hole we unconsciously
fall into over and over.

Commentary: She Dreamed It

This ten-line poem reflects a major change in perspective.

Once we detach from our identity, find the present moment, and get the witnessing presence up and running, we know for sure that we are not who we thought we were. The identity is realized to be a mental construct, not who we are.

When you wake up out of that identity into who you really are, everything changes — and nothing changes. Circumstances stay largely the same. But you are no longer the separate one efforting your way through the mystery, lobbying at every point to assert and maintain your identity. You are awake and alive within the mystery of the eternal present moment — and you flow, enacting your part, accepting what comes. You no longer resist what is. You accept events and move through them. You act when it's time to act; you rest when it's time to rest.

She Dreamed It
6-22-2007

You think
It's 'me' in here
But I know it's not

I know
Who really owns this body
My Heart has fallen from my grasp
Love owns this body

She dreamed it
She awakened it
And She is using it now

Commentary: The High End of Duality

There is a beautiful moment at the end of the
Ramayana, where Rama turns to Hanuman
and offers him 'the gift' — full absorption and
dissolution in God Consciousness. That is
considered the gold standard, the ideal in the
enlightenment traditions. But is it? Hanuman says
to Rama something like, "My Lord, I would rather
remain just a bit separate and have the joy of
serving You." Voila !!!

The High End of Duality is my agreement song with
Hanuman. The higher registers of creation are
the sweet spot in the universe. You have passed
beyond the vulnerability of your naiveté, navigated
your way through ignorance, made it through
the insanity of violence, domination and control;
you vanquished your resistance, found your Self
and your Divine Nature. Now the divine qualities
radiate from your presence and your cup runneth
over.

That is the sweet spot, not absorption. If
dissolution in God or Silence were the answer, then
why form the created worlds at all? Creation is
here for God's love of expression. God wants to BE.
God wants to create. God wants to express. And
you are not other than That.

The High End of Duality
9-3-07

The high end of duality is delicious
That's where joy abounds
That is where we dance

Passing beyond resistance
Your surrender gives you wings
Energy moves and you take flight
Gone are the ballast and tethering lines

Resistance to the truth drops away
Willingness appears
You can see the feathers forming as devotion grows

Love soooo loves
That whenever She remembers Herself
She takes flight

No longer bound by negativity
She disappears into the Light
Of Her Own Nature

All Hearts take flight when they remember themselves

Commentary: Identity

I wanted to form a seamless transition between psychology and spirituality. Psychology focuses on mind. Spirit focuses on that which is aware of the mind.

I wanted to acknowledge the wisdom of psychology's developmental stages, the movement from dependence, to independence, to interdependence and cooperation. Some transpersonal psychologists, like the wonderful team of Chuck and Lency Spezzano, also point to the next stage of development — radical dependence on God.

But I wanted to go a bit further and say as true as that is, it still carries the scent of separation. It would be more true to say the mind softens during the cooperation stage, then begins opening to the Light of its own Divine Nature as it embraces the direct experience of Spirit.

As the Light of its Being floods in, the individual begins living off that Light, because that is its life. That begins the stage of uncompromising faith, radical dependence on God.

When the separation disappears, we realize that we were always in the Heart of God.

Identity
10-11-08

Dependent!
We all arrive this way — physically dependent
As we discover our power
Dependence yields to independence

Independence is a glorious phase
We come into our power
We have function and freedom
We are distinct and individual, we express and create

Ego grows capable and strong
On its journey through separation
Like a protective shell, ego guards over
The natural evolution from dependence into independence

Yet even higher function waits just around the corner
Independence evolves into cooperation
Just look at your body, it is a symphony of
Collaboration — all higher functions require cooperation

CONTINUED >>

But it does not stop there
An even grander adventure waits
Softening the hardened shell of identity
And recognizing Witnessing Presence

Thought is not self-aware
Something is aware of it
What is that something?

Self recognition emerges
As the witnessing consciousness
Is realized to be the Source of your Being

The old word for Consciousness is Spirit
The Source of your being
The I Am presence at the core of existence

Ego softens through cooperation
Eventually receding into a secondary identity
As the Divine Life flowing through you
Is recognized as your own Deepest Self

Spirit is your Divine Nature, your primary identity
Individuation was always secondary

You are that Something
Watching the individualized self
Wrestle its way out of the cocoon of separation
Into the freedom of Being

Your destiny — is wings

Commentary: Sing Poet, Sing

During Hafiz's spiritual training, his teacher, Attar, began calling him a pregnant woman. One day Hafiz became exasperated. "Attar, why do you call me a pregnant woman?" And Attar said something like "Because you are so full of God's poems, Hafiz, that one day, when your heart opens, you will give birth to them all."

In this poem I am saying that when the poet (the individual self) becomes a mystic (open to the Spirit's Divine Nature), then Love (God) becomes your dance partner.

The poem ends with a wonderful truth.

Sing Poet, Sing
10-27-07

That is how Hafiz came to dance
In service of Attar!
Once pregnant he gave birth
A thousand times singing Her praises

Luminous birds
Would spring from his mouth
Every time
His Heart broke open

Poets become mystics
When the Divine appears
And Love
Takes up the dance

We become what we serve
So . . . sing poet, sing!

Commentary: The Pain Body

We could call the pain body by many different names. I am using the term coined by others, but made popular by Eckhart Tolle. I like the notion of the pain body behaving like an organism. It is a ball of negatively charged energy within you that needs to feed from time to time. It asserts itself into your awareness and gets you to focus negatively. Your negative response is its food. It strengthens itself with negativity and then subsides for a time.

What allows the pain body to sustain itself is lack of presence and mentalization. If you do your work, your pain body will get smaller and smaller, until it's fully healed. You will have gone a long way towards healing your mind. If you tell stories, blame and complain, your pain body will continue to feed off you, and you will continue to be a nuisance to yourself and others.

This poem arose out of a pain body attack I was having. A pain body attack leads with energy, not thought, so you feel it first. That's why it seems to arrive without warning. I noticed this attack and stayed present without believing the stories. After a while, it receded. I wanted to demonstrate how the mechanism works in a poem, how to stay present while moving through these kinds of attacks.

The Pain Body
7-24-08

Falling into the pain of loss
So achingly familiar
Each descending feeling
Each accompanying thought passing by — in free fall

But today, I am awake
And that makes all the difference
Today the pain body does not feed alone
I am with the pain — present

But the pain body
Does not like company
It prefers to dine alone
It prefers the cover of darkness

How many attacks
Have I slept through ?
How many rabbit holes
Have I fallen into ?

CONTINUED >>

But this sleep is over
For I am here — and I refuse to relinquish the now

I refuse to relinquish the moment
I refuse to go back to sleep

I am awake
And if the cost of being awake is this old pain
Then we dine together

So, today, I dine with the beast
A hauntingly familiar ache
Eyes wide open, undefended

This is the mouth of the kleshas*
And the sound of freedom
Both

* A klesha is a vulnerability that allows unconscious negative
patterns to express

Walking Through Your Mind
8-21-07

The world is not outside of you
It is inside of you
You are walking
Through your mind

Having fallen asleep
We have forgotten
Having forgotten
We suffer

It can be different, angel!

Commentary: Savitri

In *Savitri* I am suggesting a change in perspective. I am reaching out to a thousand old souls who are holding silence and dissolution in God as the goal of spiritual life. You may have made it to freedom, but are you satisfied? Are you deeply fulfilled — or can you hear the Mother's voice whispering through the silence into your ear, calling you into creation, into the dance?

Let me say this: you are not finished until you pick up the power of creation. I experienced this, but no one was talking about it. Everyone was saying "There is no me to do anything," and "Just be in the silence that you are." But no-self is not the answer, or it would be fulfilling.

Life Herself came courting, whispering, "Sonjan, come play, come dance. Might we turn this world into paradise together?" So this is the gift I have for you: bring your silence and come dance.

Savitri is an acknowledgement of Sri Aurobindo's immense perspective in <u>Savitri, a Legend and a Symbol</u> in which he describes the personage Savitri as "the Divine World, daughter of the Sun, goddess of the supreme Truth who comes down and is born to save."

When I use the word Savitri, I mean one who is initiated into the Solar Lineage or one whose development is such that they listen for and embody divine intention in lieu of their own agenda.

Savitri
6-5-08

Silence is not the goal
It is the medium through which creation flows

It's as if silence were space itself – empty, aware
Space
And that Space summoned forth creation into Itself
As Itself, and that Space were conscious
And self-aware, the silent observer of all that is

Everything occurring within Itself

All creation exists within this Space
Where else could it exist?
Silence and creation are not two
They are One dancing

As if Space Itself were the Ultimate Perceiver
Pure conscious awareness, aware of Itself
And within its empty Self it summons creation
In a lusty cascade of descending frequencies

So, sweet meditators, when you discover silence
As you must, you might be only half way Home

CONTINUED >>

Yes, you have discovered the Homeland
You have discovered yourself as Silence —
perceiving

But that Self
Wants to dance
Wants to express
Wants to create

The game has only just begun
Your self-recognition
Opens the door
To the dance of paradise

The Divine Intention is
To bring forth paradise
In ever descending frequencies
Within the forming worlds

You are that Silence
Come to dance
Here within your Self
As this forming world

Pick up the trumpet
And sound your Divine Nature

Sing your song
Dance your dance

There is no need to park yourself in silence
You are the Silence
Beckoning Itself into expression

Who else is there?
You are the dancers
You are the polished white stones
Who have come to dance

Mystery School

A mystery school has two aspects: 1] it is a teaching environment where the knowledge of the elusive mysteries of life are taught, and 2] the knowledge is held in confidence, available to initiated members and not part of the public record. The knowledge is esoteric, intended only for the initiated.

Most churches are exoteric; their teachings are fully disclosed and available to the public. In contrast, the Mormon Church is esoteric; only a qualifying member has access to the temple wisdom. In a mystery school, you have to join the school to gain access to the knowledge.

"Proprietary" is a term used in business to mean much of the same thing. Essentially . . . it's a secret. It's in-house knowledge, not available to the public.

The Masonic Lodge, fraternal orders, college fraternities, etc. all hold secrets available only to members, but their primary purpose is as service or social organizations, not the teaching of wisdom. Guilds also hold secrets and teach, but their focus is teaching a skill or craft, not the mysteries of life. A mystery school teaches the mysteries of life and keeps its wisdom private.

Why would anyone want to keep secrets, especially wisdom secrets? You have but to look at our history to see the madness society besets on those who wander outside the accepted box; Galileo, Calpurnius, Martin Luther, Jesus of Nazareth, to name a few notables. Society's knee-jerk response to differences is persecution. Mystery schools have evolved from antiquity as a way of side stepping persecution.

More importantly is the issue of purity, to keep the knowledge pure and intact for posterity. If a teaching is made public, like Christianity, people create offshoots, like Protestantism, and the offshoots create offshoots and on it goes until you have a hundred variations. People take the part of the original teaching that they like, add it to whatever else they believe and package it into a new teaching, some of which is true, some of which is not true. The original teaching gets degraded. Teachers take a bit of this and a smattering of that and it becomes the newest teachers' training.

Packagers serve an important function, but purity is not one of them. Mystery schools on the other hand are not generally variations or knockoffs of something else; they are the original fountainhead of inspired mystical information.

To maintain the purity of that wisdom, mystery schools require their members to become stewards of the knowledge. The initiates protect the knowledge, honor it and keep it sacred. They don't knock a chunk off, mix it with their other knowledge and present it to the market as their latest product. They protect the knowledge and keep it sacred. They teach from within the school.

"We do not lose our individuality;

we gain our universality.

The drop does not dissolve in the Ocean,

the Ocean enters the drop."

Sonjan's Story and the Solar Lineage, pg 118

Prakash
9-23-07

There is a light
That flows like honey
To the awakened Heart

Drenched in nectar
Soaked in bliss
Why would anyone not ask?
Why would anyone not open to Her?

Beckon Love, call out, yield
Ask Her to come
Forever . . . ask Her to come

Commentary: Cavorting With Mira

This is a fun poem. It refers to Mirabai, the famous ecstatic Indian/Persian poet who was married to the king of the region. She became a royal queen, but lost favor for studying with a guru of the untouchable caste. She ran away and became a wandering ecstatic, reciting her mystical poems from town to town. She is known for these poems and her outrageous ways.

This joy poem has Mira's footprints all over it. It even has the constable in it, reflecting her years of running from the king's men, who were trying to find and punish her. *Cavorting With Mira* is a conversation between the town deputy and the constable. The deputy is reporting a disturbance in the market square. There is a poet in the market who is drunk on the Divine (the wine made only in the heart) and is creating a nuisance. But the mood is catching on; people are starting to join in and play.

It is really a conversation between two points of view: the rational world of the ego-mind with its insistence on structure, following the rules and behaving, and the world of Spirit, of Divine Nature, where love and joy rule and God is celebrated as the obvious reality.

Cavorting With Mira
7-25-07

"We have news of a local nuisance, sir
A poet is wandering through the village
Drunk on the wine
Made only in the Heart

"The singing and dancing
Are becoming a nuisance
People are gathering
Shops are closing

"He is cavorting with Mira
They are dancing in the stalls and the street
But no one can see her
No one hears her

"The joy is intoxicating
Others are joining the dance
The Friend is here
Someone saw Hafiz just a moment ago

CONTINUED >>

"So please, constable,
Before this gets out of hand
Talk to the boy rationally
Bring him back to the real world"

But the poet is heard shouting back
"This joy IS the real world
You must be living in shadows
If this joy does not grow wings on your back
And set you free"

A Good Mind
2-22-07

If it's love, it doesn't hurt
If it's obligation, it's not love
It's a story you bought from the mind
The Heart will not harm

Love is uplifting and allowing
Mind is linear and rational
A good mind serves the Heart
An unruly mind serves itself

The vulnerability of God is this:
When God enters expression
Oneness is forgotten

In duality
The mind steps forward
To define us
And the lights go out

Commentary: Running From Emptiness

Have you ever searched for a pencil, only to find it behind your ear, or looked for your glasses and found them on your head?

In our disconnection, we run from emptiness. We keep ourselves busy. We focus on content. We stay in our mind and away from the void. We are afraid of it. In those years or lifetimes we run from emptiness, but when the fog lifts, we discover that it is exactly in silence where we find ourselves and our bliss.

Emptiness is a notion that comes from the mental perspective. It means empty of content, nothing for the mind to recognize or perceive, without attributes. But that is a mental interpretation. What Spirit sees in that emptiness is silence, presence, bliss, awareness. It's where you find the Self.

The irony is we were running away from the very thing we were looking for. Peace and equanimity, harmony and love were right there all the time.

Running From Emptiness
7-9-2000

Who'd have thought?
We just had no idea
Where the Soul lived

How many lifetimes
Did we run from that emptiness?
Only to discover that in meeting it
The emptiness becomes a fountain of joy

The Soul discovers Itself
As the present moment
And the joy
Begins

Commentary: Prodigal Son: A Poem for Warriors, Saviors and other Crusaders

Mahatma Gandhi, champion of the people and master of social reform, approached the renowned mystic Ramana Maharshi and said something like "Hey Ramana, it would sure be nice if you would come out of the ashram and help me wrestle our country back from the British." To which the mystic replied, "My job is silence."

Different people are born for different reasons: some come to change the world; some come to change themselves; some come to give, others come to take.

The crusader, the social advocate, the archetype of the warrior work to make the world a better place, and the world certainly needs the help. But the fundamental change that comes to a society is a change in consciousness. Raise the consciousness, open the heart and you change the world.

This poem calls to all the noble warriors intent on changing the world for the better.

Prodigal Son:
A Poem for Warriors, Saviors and other Crusaders
11-18-08

You want to change the world
And that is a beautiful thing
But, could you be making a fundamental error?
Are you changing the real world
Or throwing stones at a mirror?

All your focus and energy are here in the natural world
But, crusader, is this really the world you think it is?

Ask yourself "Is this world self-aware
Or is there something aware of it?"
If there is something aware of it
Then what is that something?

Yes, this world is real enough, but it is also an illusion
That's not a denial of its reality
It means it is not what it appears to be
This world is reflective

CONTINUED >>

Why is everything we experience as solid
Composed of atoms, known to be empty?

Why does something so empty appear so solid?
If this question does not intrigue you, even a little

Then slowly turn away from this poem and
Return to your world changing
Because the illusion is not yet done with you and
The world needs so much help

For it is in the dream
That we develop our skills
Our power to create positively
Our ability to feel joy coursing through our veins

But there is a time for waking up
If this question intrigues you
Then perhaps this is your time — your time to stop
Changing the world and start changing yourself

There is a deeper Self
Which is calling you through the illusion
Calling you back to your Self

Is it time for the prodigal son to come home?
Only you can say

Only One of us Here
3-26-06

The world is a projection
A hologram of thought
A symphony in the key of two
We see "the other" as the problem

It's set up that way
Ego needs an enemy
Needs a position
Needs something to push against

Wake up — it's a mirror, silly!!!
You are looking at your self

There is only One of us here
One being
One mind
One forgotten reality

Commentary: Sacred Food

This is a fun poem in which the Mother is playing with me, reminding me that love is everything. She is keeping me on track. She is telling me not to take myself too seriously.

She says, "Sonjan, drowning in love is your only job."

It reminds me of one of my favorite Rumi poems:

An intellectual is all the time showing off
Lovers dissolve and become bewildered

Intellectuals try not to drown
While the whole purpose of love
Is drowning

Sacred Food
7-26-08

Ahhhh . . . Venus is here
That lovely, lovely Divine Wench
Whispering in my ear: "Love is everything!"

She says: "Forget your ramblings, sweet Sonjan.
Drowning in love is your only job"

She whispers: "Until the Heart opens,
There is no sacred food, no dharma"
How do we sustain life without the sacred?
Badly ! ! !

She says:
You were meant to feed on love
I designed you so
Love is your sustaining food

All else
Is drawn from that
All else — comes from that

Commentary: Discernment

Discrimination is the power that the mind truly has. It is your power. But it must be informed by the heart. The beautiful life work of Byron Katie is a testament to this truth.

What woke up in Katie was the Divine Nature, the witnessing presence, the heart. It changed everything.

But she still had to deal with her crazy mind. And that is what we all have to deal with. The way Home winds through the valley of listening, discernment and discrimination.

Discernment
12-16-07

You are in a creation field
Desires manifest, thoughts become reality
Whether you like it or not

If you believe your thoughts to be true
Without asking your Heart
You will blame others and miss your Beautiful Self

If you hold on to your beliefs instead of your Heart
You will find fault in others and miss the door to heaven

Stand in the moment and ask each thought
 "Is this true? Is this thought true?"
Snuggle up to that big beautiful mind of yours and
whisper "Sweetheart, HOW do you know if that
thought is true? "

Your Heart will tell you in the silent langue of the
Soul Then you discern. You listen and discern
Your choice to listen and discern
Is the road Home

Commentary: River of Wine

Here is another "river of wine" poem.
What can I say? Guilty as charged!

You will find me under the Divine Waterfall
with the rest of the intoxicated lovers.

River of Wine
7-6-2000

There is such pleasure
In opening to the Spirit
You have no idea
Or you would have entered It years ago

When the Spirit acquires you
The real joy begins
A magnetic resonance
Fills you

Call it Presence
Or the Holy Spirit
Or the Mother
Who cares?

When you live as This
The whole world is full
You have found the river of wine

Commentary: Passion for the Sacred

This hot passionate poem says: all your practices and techniques are useless if you don't open your heart. Technical efficiency is not going to do it.

Everything on the spiritual path relies on your heart being open. Everything!

If your heart is open, you will feel the love, which is embodied in the metaphor of the swan: Love flying home to Itself. Love is your instructor, your coach, your mentor, your guide, your own Essential Nature.

Passion for the Sacred
7-4-08

Passion for the Sacred
Will grow wings on your back
And open up the heavens

Why bend your back?
Why practice your kriyas?
Why bang out your mantras?
If your heart is not open, nothing else matters

If you are not passionate about the sacred
Then ASK, pilgrim, ask!
Get down on your knees
And pray for the door to open

Brothers, sisters
There is Light
Flooding down from Above
Open your hearts and receive

CONTINUED >>

But, sweetheart, if your heart IS open
Then you know
That there is a swan living there
Yearning to fly home to God

Set Her free!
Let Her wings become your own
She will enliven your practices
She will show you the secret ways, no one else knows

She is your Swan, your Love
Your way Home
Her beating heart
Is the sound of your breath

Relationship with Yourself
4-8-06

There are lots of courses out there
That help you improve your relationship with yourself
And I'm sure they're all good

But think about it for a moment:
Relationship with yourself?
This is the split mind at work
Creating separation

You don't have a relationship with yourself
You ARE yourself
Relationship requires two

This is one relationship that ends
When you realize who you are

Commentary: The Sugar Merchant

I was feeling such gratitude for having cracked the code on resistance and finding the art of no-effort, the art of allowing. I was feeling playful and fun and free. In this poem I just started singing, "How did I get so lucky ?

The fifth stanza tells the whole story; I stopped resisting life.

I love the final stanza, where sugar becomes the metaphor for allowing. It's playful and yet so true. The metaphor completes by referring to one who teaches the way of allowing — as a sugar merchant.

The Sugar Merchant
4-18-08

I may be more of a handful than you imagined
Still simmering here in the fire
Vulnerable — at times disappointed
Experiencing the full catastrophe of being human

Singing from within the pain
Dancing with the suffering
Opening, opening, opening

How is it that I got so lucky
As to "get" no resistance to the truth
How is it I was given this blessing of nirodha?

Here is my guess: the constant beatings
Were too much . . . and I surrendered

Now I pour the sugar of allowing
On what life brings me
And you say, Sonjan
You are becoming a sugar merchant

* Nirodha means a ceasing of all effort

The Terror of Annihilation
Commentary: The Pitcher Has Broken

In the spring of 1992, Arjuna came to Orcas Island. He was fresh from Papaji's ashram and he was on fire. He gave satsang for a week. During that week I realized that this could be it; this could be the end of me.

I knew in my heart that this teaching was capable of annihilating me. Fear exploded. What I didn't know at the time, was that the "me" that was on the chopping block, was the false identification of a separate self. I just knew that I was terrified.

When we get close to the real moment of authentic cracking open of the ego identity to the Divine Nature, fear arises — fear of losing control, fear of annihilation, of not existing anymore. For me it was terror.

You can conceptualize this till the cows come home, but when the real moment arrives, when the ego sees that opening completely to the Divine is what is being offered, it gets scared. That was my experience.

I went to Arjuna and revealed my fear. He simply asked: "Do you want to know the Truth?" I was stunned. What a profound question.

Did my identity want to continue to promote and defend itself, or was the Truth more interesting?

I had to go in my center, and there, in my deepest heart, I found the willingness to open, to open to whatever the Truth might be. Yes, I wanted to know the Truth.

The reward for that willingness came five years later and is embodied in the next poem:
The Pitcher Has Broken

"When the Spirit acquires you

the real joy begins

A magnetic resonance fills you,

Call it Presence or the Holy Spirit

Or Consciousness Itself. Who cares?

When you live as THIS the whole world is full !

You have found the River of Wine"

River of Wine, pg 201

The Pitcher Has Broken
6-16-2000

For breakfast, tears
For lunch, being moved
All night — longing

Breakfast comes
No one is here
The pitcher has broken
During the long night

Now the water
Is with Itself

Commentary: The Mother Has a Gift for You

I wrote this poem to a sweetheart.

I wanted to light the candle of recognition in her heart.

The Mother Has a Gift for You
2-23-08

The Mother has a gift for you
Hidden here in my heart
She wants to recognize Herself — as you

She longs for Her love
To flow through your chest
Yearns for Her wisdom
To take up residence in your beautiful mind

Look in the mirror
Who is looking back at you?
That is She looking at you
She — looking at Herself

I have a gift for you
From the Mother
Look in my eyes, and
See Her looking at Herself

Commentary: The Fall

It is a teaching poem, which is to say it's more teaching than poem. I wanted to define the fall of consciousness, to take it out of the clouds of abstraction and put it clearly on paper where we can look at it. It is meant to shift your perception. The poem defines the fall of consciousness, shows how we got here, and then presents the elegant path of return — not as a path of pursuit, but as a path of recognition.

The solution is not to go somewhere, but to let go of the perceived illusion.

The Fall
4-7-06

The mind is an instrument of perception
Its function is to serve Spirit
However, mind is capable of wandering off
And perceiving itself as separate

This is "The Fall"

In separation our mind becomes mortal
Seeing itself "in" a body
Confusing itself "with" a body
Now all hell breaks loose

The mind, having denied the Source
Loses function
Loses happiness, loses peace
Poor mind, poor you

Perceiving itself as separate
Mind feels alone, helpless, and vulnerable
Hiding out in a body

CONTINUED >>

Here is the problem:
Having cut itself off from Source
Mind sees everything as "two", as opposites
This is the source of conflict!

It now tries to reconcile duality
Good and evil, body and mind, you and me
But that's a dead man's game
It cannot be done

The problem is that separation is an illusion!
There is no reconciling duality!
It's an illusion, a dream
You can't solve a problem that doesn't exist

Herein, you have the world that you see before you

The solution is to recognize
That you are not separate
Not vulnerable, not helpless
And never were

The solution is to realize
That the problem never existed

A Place Like No Place
5-26-2000

Come . . .
Let me show you
Where to rest

There is a place
Which is like no place
Just here
Just now

Resting in this moment
Awareness
Tastes Its own nature
And explodes in joy

Come, let me show you
Where to rest
Just here
Just now

Commentary: Deeper Information

This poem presents the idea that there is a deeper flow of information, not available to the mind. To reach it we must go into our hearts and feel. Only feeling will unlock the code.

The intellect operates on a different frequency and will not and cannot read it. When we shift into feeling mode, our awareness blends with the energy and the information reveals itself.

If we insist on staying conceptual, we never gain access to the unbelievably rich world of wisdom embedded within energy.

Deeper Information
6-7-08

If you want deeper information than the mind can vessel
Tether your mind to the breath
Until it stops wandering

Or, chant the names of God
Until the frequency quiets the mind
Or, ask the mystic's question, "Who am I?"
And go looking without the mind

Whatever way becomes you
Must yield the gift of silence
For it is in silence that your ears begin to grow

There is a river of information
Moving through the Heart
What you seek is here
Embedded in that energy

Feeling unlocks the code
Through no medium but itself
The song hidden in your heart
Reveals the way, one delicious moment at a time

Mindfulness, Pivoting and Embracing

Mindfulness means being present in the here and now moment, aware. You are present with open awareness, not lost in thought.

Pivoting is a term used to describe the act of shifting your focus away from negative content. It is about what you think. When you find yourself thinking a negative thought, use your discrimination to shift your focus. To do this you must be mindful; you must be sufficiently present in the moment to notice that you are having thoughts. It is managing your focus. You simply pivot your awareness to something else.

Embracing is something entirely different. It does just the opposite. Embracing turns into the issue and feels it completely with undefended awareness. It uses the power of consciousness.

Awareness dissolves all lower frequencies within it. It is the power of consciousness. If you hold presence, any content, be it emotion or thought that arises, will fall away if you stay present in awareness. The field of presence (consciousness) is the most powerful element in the universe. It is who you are. Your focus is your lens for that field of awareness.

Embracing is the art of allowing thoughts, feelings and sensations to rest in your open field of awareness without resistance. Knowing when to pivot and when to embrace is an art that requires mindfulness, presence, and awareness.

Pivoting is good for thoughts — impressions that are just passing by in the mind. It is easy just to turn away from a passing negative thought and that's probably 95 percent of all negativity, just ambient ideas in the collective river of thought.

However, if you dwell on a thought long enough, the thought begins to gather energy around it. It actually develops an energy body of its own. It begins growing an energetic tail. It gathers similar thoughts to it and they band together to form a conglomerate. It now enters the unconscious as an energy package, and when it reappears it will likely express as a feeling, as a signature of energy, rather than as a thought. So it is already inside your feeling nature before you think it.

What I have found is that any thought that has progressed to the stage of having an energy root cannot simply be pivoted away from. It now carries more energy than you. At this point you need to abandon any attempt to turn away from the thought (pivoting) and enter it directly and consciously (embracing). You didn't catch it earlier when it was a random thought, so now you are going to have to go deeper into your nature and be present in full awareness to get at the energy of it.

To do this, become the student and let the ball of thought-energy become your teacher. What is it telling you? What does it have to say? If you listen to the energy of it, the information will begin to communicate with you. It is usually a place in your life where you said NO to life and stopped the energy. By listening you can return to the YES and heal.

Be aware of "stories" during this process. The mind can collapse your field of presence through mentalizing you within a story, like, "This shouldn't be happening," or "It's all his fault." If you are not mindful, such thinking will go unnoticed and the field of presence will collapse and you will have to return to presence. It is the field of presence that does the work. Stay mindful.

Buddha Nature
5-5-2000

Buddha Nature

You can't find it by looking
The search just hides it
You can't avoid it by running
The addictions consume you

But relax, just here, just now
And there It is
Colorless, odorless, tasteless Presence
Your Original Nature

Commentary: The Song of Separation

I wrote this poem to a friend who was trying so hard to be good, to live purely, to find God. Her diligence and fortitude were amazing. She worked so hard. She could have made the Augean Stables look good.

We were in an intense dialogue around separation, duty, obligation, and effort and struggle when this poem came through. She was philosophically aligned with the transformation into effortlessness, but actualizing it challenges a lifetime of thinking.

This poem is a mix of playful elements like, "I am a thief here on the Mother's business" and deeply serious notions such as, "When you punish yourself you're punishing God."

You can't talk someone out of being separate. The identity is deep and abiding. We doggedly hold on to our ideas of who we think we are. However, if we don't separate our selves from God in the first place, then we don't have to claw our way back. If you don't take the first trip into separation, then no return journey is needed.

When it comes to God, don't be penny-wise and pound-foolish.

The Song of Separation
3-14-08

You stay away from sugar
You do not eat meat
You drink green tea
All the time looking for God

You wouldn't have to look so hard
If you didn't separate yourself in the first place
She would simply be everywhere

Yet you hang on to this notion of separation
Like a hungry dog
Any suggestion that YOU might be divine
Is met with howls of "blasphemy"

You insist you are separate
Even though you stole this thought from God
Tied it around your ankle
And ran headlong into the dream

You are a thief complaining of booty
You sing like a wounded song bird
Lamenting separation

CONTINUED >>

Wake up, sweetheart
You are walking through your own mind
Dragging this lie with you
Like a lifeless doll

You hold on to this idea that you are not the Divine
That you are not She, dipped in flesh
That you are some "something"
That you haven't quite figured out yet

Well, it has been figured out
You are God, my dear
The eternal beloved of the Mother
The prize of your Father

Okay, you are not ALL of God
You are a facet, an expression, a Divine perspective
So perhaps we could say, a Godling
But God, nonetheless!

Don't use this individuality as a diminishment
The mind is such a trickster
It chews on the bones of separation
Then buries them in your back yard

I am here on the Mother's business — a thief
She asked me to steal this mad idea away from you

And return it to Her
Before anyone else gets hurt

This "I" that looks in the mirror
This individualized self
IS the expression of the Divine
You are She

Yet you insist this is you
This is not you !!!!
This is the Mother looking through Her eyes
Which you image to be you

I am sorry that you got such bad advice from your
Parents and all the thieves living here in paradise
But that doesn't change the truth

When you are angry at yourself
You are angry at God !
When you punish yourself
You are punishing God

I hope you surrender gracefully
As I tease you, love you, cajole you
All the while wrestling this tiny mad thought
From your grasp

"All attempts to control Love

Are attempts to control God"

Divine Lovers p.137

When The Mind Stops Whining
4-25-06

It is the mind that needs healing
When this mind stops whining about being separate
These broken wings mend and we fly

Being is an Ocean of Infinite Potential
But forget your Essential Nature
And you're back on the ground

Heal this wounded mind
By forgiving the world
For all the mistakes — that you made

Commentary: The Comforter is Here

When I use the term the "Friend", I am borrowing from the Sufi poets who use the term the Friend to refer to the Divine, to God. It carries intimacy and affection. It reminds me of the Christian reference to the Comforter, which embodies the feeling that you are loved, that the Divine cares for you and loves you in a personal way, and is here right now to help with anything and everything.

This isn't the vengeful God of the Old Testament This is the God of Love. This is the wonderful God who whispers in your ear, "Sweetheart, what wonderful mischief shall we get into together today?"

I use capitalization to refer to the Divine, to the Transcendent. It's my code to signal that we are talking about the Divine. If a verse reads, "sweetheart" it indicates a person is being addressed, but when I say "what shall we do Sweetheart?" it is the Divine being addressed. When I say "You" or "She" or "Her" or "Him" I am addressing the Divine.

I use the word Shine to indicate the Light of God, which I capitalize. When I capitalize Love, I am addressing Love as the essence of the Divine. I also capitalize Life, because Life is sacred. It is the expression the divine.

The Comforter is Here
4-8-06

Turn that sadness over to the Friend
Why manage it on your own?
Let the Beloved nestle
Her love-wings around you

The reason that raw nerve aches
Is because you forgot who you are
Your amnesia cuts you deeply
An aching separatencss

You ache because you refuse to open
This refusal to love is killing you
Let go — let the Comforter in
And be loved

Commentary: The Big Lie

This was an important poem for me. It had been brewing for years. I had passed through the big lie, the dream story that keeps separation working. The trance was broken. I could now see.

The curtain had been pulled back and there was a culture, operating a Ponzi scheme here in the land of separation, selling a story that had entranced a world. In the story, a few appear to be winning, while the rest are snared in struggle and effort.

The truth was running quietly in the background, but only understood by those who had already come through the process and pierced the veil.

Understanding this changes your worldview.

The Big Lie
3-26-06

Duality is a wild dance of opposites
Ego forms within the mind
And crafts a "you" and a "me"
A "here" and "there"

It wants the adventure of
Bullying itself over us
On its way to getting from here to there
It's an elaborate dance requiring judgment and conflict

But really, what's the point?
The cost of separation is suffering
This is the big lie:
Separation was never set up to work
It was set up to suffer

Duality is a no-holds-barred adventure
Designed to get you stuck
Sooooo deeply in the muck of negativity
That only the Divine can extricate you

CONTINUED >>

Like the tar baby
Each blow against negativity
Only gets you more stuck in it

When you are so mired
That you hit bottom
When there is nowhere else to turn
Only then, do we turn towards the unknown God

Think about it: if separation worked, really worked
Who would wake up from the dream?
Even saints would sleep
It is only because separation hurts
That we find our way Home

Only when we open to the luminous possibility
That there is a God
And that He is on our side
And that His creation is also on our side

Only then are we lifted
That is the paradigm shift
That is where our eyes open
And paradise appears

One Eye on God
11-17-07

Keep one eye on God
And the other eye on Life
The human experience
Is supposed to be bathed in Light

You have to live it to know it
So let it come — all of it

Summon the courage
To experience your experience
Awake and undefended
Let Life fill the eye of your experience

God is watching
With the other eye

Commentary: The Sugar and the Pain

There is so much to say about this poem. A whole book could be written on it: The Power of Consciousness.

How do we respond to the life force moving through us? The primary response I see is when the life force moves strongly we go into the mind and suppress the energy. We shut it down. We turn it off. Over time, this makes us solid. We are saying "No" to life. We develop a stone in our vital center.

The second approach is just the opposite; it is the strategy of exaggerated expression. Instead of moving into the mind and suppressing, we enter the vitality of the energy body and express wildly. We let both barrels loose. We let it fly. If you grew up in a Latin culture, you probably saw lots of this.

Both are strategies to handle energy, feeling and emotion. But what if there were a third approach that wasn't suppressive or expressive, that wasn't even a strategy? If we could simply BE with the energy moving through us, instead of expressing or suppressing it, but just experience it deeply, through being open and allowing to the flow, then another possibility opens up.

First, the energy begins to reveal to you the information contained within it. Energy is a stream of information, but you must be willing to feel it in order to read it. You read it by blending with it, which requires willingness, openness, and presence.

Additionally, the power of consciousness comes into play. Awareness is the most powerful force in the universe and the highest frequency. The law of resonant fields says the strongest frequency will prevail and set the resonance when two vibrations meet.

The clearest example of this is the tuning fork. When struck, the tuning fork will have a higher frequency, but a coffee table has more mass and quickly brings the vibration of the fork down to its level.

This would change if a power source were applied to the tuning fork that caused it to maintain its frequency; the table would then vibrate up to the tuning fork's frequency.

Consciousness, as the *highest* frequency, also becomes the *strongest* frequency when you are consciously present as awareness. Your presence is the power source that makes the difference. No lower vibration, such as a negative emotion, can maintain its frequency, its essence, if you are consciousness, present and open.

It's as if life were playing the rock-paper-scissors game with you, and your awake presence trumps everything, all the time, when you are present.

In the poem, I say it this way, let the emotion be your teacher. This requires you to be present and receptive. Now you are in the sweet spot of allowing awareness to blend with the emotion, and the emotion disappears every time. That is why experiencing your emotions, without suppressing or expressing them, is the elegant path. You experience their essence and they disappear.

You must stay present, however. If the mind seduces you into thinking, your field of presence will collapse and the frequency of the emotion can reappear. The mind will offer ideas and stories about why this "shouldn't be happening" or who is at fault. If you fall into that delusion, you mentalize your self. Very few people have cultured the ability to be present while thinking.

Consciousness acts like a solvent to dissolve all frequencies lower than its own nature. The divine qualities, however, expand in the presence of awareness because divine qualities, such as love and gratitude, are attributes of consciousness, while emotions are a distortion of divine qualities.

Patience is a divine quality. Impatience is an emotion. Gratitude is a divine quality, while envy is an emotion. Love is a divine quality. Hate is an emotion. Do you get the sense of it?

Divine qualities thrive in the presence of awareness. Being present to love causes love to swell and expand. Appreciation begets more appreciation. Dwelling on gratitude can become a rampage of divine energy moving within you.

In the poem, I say YOU are the sugar, the sweetness of consciousness. Once you show up, everything changes.

Experiencing emotional energy directly without suppression or dramatized expression is the elegant path, but don't make a strategy out of it. If you become present as a strategy with the goal of making something go away, you lose your innocence. You trade your openness for a goal.

The objective turns you into a warrior instead of an investigator. Enter with innocence, with your openness intact. Be an explorer, an investigator of reality, a sleuth for the truth. Let the life force be your teacher and you will become the student of Life Herself.

"If you stay in your mind

You'll miss it all"

What Is Now? Pg 289

Sugar and the Pain
4-8-08

Show up
For this sadness
It is your teacher

Show up and be present
Feel it deeply
Taste it within your being

Don't go back to sleep
There is information waiting for you
Within that sadness

You retrieve it by reading it
Listen and feel
Savor the subtleties
Be a luminous investigator

Once YOU are there
The sugar has arrived
Your awake presence
Sets everything free

Commentary: Believers Say

As the ship sails over the horizon, it is lost to our view. But from the ship's perspective, it is arriving at a new view point, which can no longer be seen by those ashore.

This poem expresses just such a transition. Belief is an activity of mind, in which we hold something to be true or false until we know for sure, at which time there is no further need for the belief. We know.

Belief is a transition tool, like a map or a menu. It guides us.

When a believer actually hears or feels the force of the Living God, they put the belief down and start following the Call. From the perspective of their fellow comrades, however, this is seen as a betrayal of faith. In reality, it is just the opposite. Someone has finally put the menu down and has turned their attention to the meal, which has just arrived.

If you don't respond to the Call, the luminosity in your life goes out.

Believers Say
2-8-2000

When the inner ear
Hears the word of God for the first time
It turns and starts walking
Towards the Sacred One

The believers gather
And say
"How sad, she has lost her faith
She no longer believes"

It's always this way!
God calls Himself to Himself
One by one

Believers become mystics
When they turn inward
And start the journey
Home

Beyond Belief

There in nothing in this book that I ask you
to believe; rather, I invite you into your own
experience. That is where true learning occurs.

We all have an inner teacher inside who knows,
if we have the patience to listen. The leap from
believing in others to listening for ourselves
requires courage. We have to know that we can
listen and discern.

As you move through this book, feel the poems.
If one doesn't feel right, put it aside. When it does
feel right, embrace it as your own truth, not mine.
Embrace it because you resonate with it. Own it
as your own truth.

The truth is easier to hear than you might think.
Everyone has the ability to discern whether an
idea or thought feels good or bad. Begin there.
This simple act becomes the practice of choosing
Life. This is the underlying principle: Life feels
good.

Some truths are universal and others are
provisional, in that they are only partially true.
It's like saying water comes from the faucet. While
that's true as far as it goes, it's a provisional truth
because there is so much more to the story. Don't
believe any of this — instead open and listen.

Awakening
3-31-2000

In the mind
Everything is two
In the Self
Everything is One

The difference — awakening

Commentary: Red Eyes

When speaking the divine language, it is initiated ever more softly until it is not even spoken in the mind. This is a vibrational language. You follow the vibration, like a thread, through the mind, through silence, through the unconscious, into its source in the expanse.

The territory being entered is so subtle that thought is left behind, impressions are left behind, even silence is left behind.

For me, it feels like exploring the edge between where I exist, and where I don't exist. The Oneness is so vast that the mind cannot expand to meet It. I refer to it as the truth expanse.

The Sarvamahat poem details this experience, but before reaching that expanse, there is a moment of unconscious, a period of blinking off of recognizable consciousness. The beauty of mantra is that the vibration carries consciousness through that unconscious leg and out the other side into the truth expanse.

Before entering the experience described in the *Sarvamahat*, I had the experience described here in *Red Eyes*. I was in the unconscious leg having this experience of a dark being with red eyes. But instead of being afraid, I was giving him satsang.

I was encouraging him to remember the Light. I was giving him love. Then I whooshed upward and entered the Sarvamahat experience.

The seed tones in the divine language become the vibration you follow through the mind, through silence and out beyond the mind into the truth expanse. On the day of this poem, that journey passed through Red Eye's neighborhood.

"Like the tar baby,

each blow against negativity

only gets you more stuck in it"

The Big Lie, pg 233

Red Eyes
12-27-08

They came somehow in deep meditation
And sat me down

Sitting across the table from his red eyes
Giving him satsang
"Oh dark being, crushed angel, fallen beloved
You remember the Shine, don't you?

"Your nature too is Light
Here, have some love
Remember when you were Light?
That's all I'm talking about"

The scene narrows and fades
Until only his red eyes remain
At the end of a disappearing tunnel
I am being lifted into samadhi

POP . . . I am in the truth expanse, immobile
Impressions floating by
As quiet as snowfall

Commentary: Apprenticeship of the Soul

This is the Soul talking about how it began incarnating a million years ago and the developmental stages it has gone through.

For me, it carries the same ring of eternity as that sweet moment in Conversations with God, where the little soul goes to God and says: "I want to know myself." And God says something like, "Then take upon your self the darkness," -- meaning, incarnate into duality and find your way Home. This is dimensional Soul talk.

Half the adventure passes by before the Soul realizes that there is more to life than survival. This is a huge turning point in the evolution of a Soul. Then more millennia slip by before the Soul is able the "feel" God through the density of the flesh. Finally it reaches the milestone of knowing God to be inside.

The poem ends with the Soul's return to innocence. You can hear the wisdom and the love that have been gained as the Soul whispers into God's ear.

Apprenticeship of the Soul
4-19-2000

A thousand thousand years ago
I came here
To try my hand
At being human

Five thousand centuries passed before I saw
There was more to life than survival
Another thousand centuries
Before I could actually "feel" You

Thousands more years slipped by
Before I found You — inside

This life is our dancing love affair
Finding You and merging into Us!
How do I tell them, Sweetheart
How beautiful they are?

Commentary: Invitation to an Angel

As you draw close to an angel, the beauty is upwelling. They live on Light and their joy is in giving. The more gratitude you feel, the more these beings are drawn by your presence.

A moment of appreciation and beauty began welling up and this poem came spilling out. I was invoking angels. I was asking angels to come make their home here with me, in my heart, in my home. My life was lifting higher and higher and my home was becoming a temple. I wanted to dwell with these magnificent beings in sacred space.

The poem is my call to them: "Come, let us live together in space made sacred by love, generosity and gratitude." I adore the line "the warm brush of your wing" — it carries such affection and intimacy. This is an intimate, personal calling-out poem to the angels.

Invitation to an Angel
7-27-08

Sweet lovers of Light
Servants of the Father
Lovers of the Mother
Beings of Light

Your presence ignites the Soul
Your beauty brings tears to my eyes
The warm brush of your wing
Sends my Heart soaring

Come, make your home so near to me
That the rose is your face smiling
That the beauty of this house
Is your luminous kiss

Sacred presence
A corridor between worlds
An interdimensional alliance of loving
Generosity and gratitude

That the beauty that you are
Be the treasure of this house

Commentary: Send the Guards Home

Once the mind perceives something, it stores it in memory. Thereafter, it no longer references the thing itself, but the memory of the thing. Over time, it becomes harder and harder to enter the now moment innocently because mental referencing has taken its place.

We end up living in our minds and losing our ability to open to the reality of the present moment.

I was having lunch with such a person. She was very smart, but she could not see the obvious; she was not present in the moment. She was brilliant within the bandwidth she was working — the mind — but she could not access the moment, except from her mental perspective.

I was just present with her, loving her. She was talking about intimacy and whether to let people into her life. I was beckoning her into the moment, into her beautiful heart. She could not see that I was already in her heart.

This poem came the next day as a response to our conversation. It's really a conversation between two different perspectives, the heart and the mind.

Send the Guards Home
5-19-2000

You think you are looking at me
But only the body is out here
If you want to see me — turn around
Look inside

Your defenses are useless here, my dear
Stop looking out over the fortifications
Of your walled city

I am already inside the compound
Inside the Holy Chambers
Inside the very Throne Room of your Heart
Adoring your Beloved Self

Send the guards home
And meet me here
In the sweetness
Of your Essential Natural

Commentary: Pain versus Suffering

This was a revelation for me. I finally understood. Suffering is all in the mind. It is not in "what is" but in our reaction to what is. When we tell stories like "This shouldn't be happening," or "It's all his fault," we add a layer of interpretation in the mind, which causes us mental pain. That is the suffering.

Pain in the physiology is an important part of the design. We need to know when something is too hot or too cold to touch, when hunger pangs tell us to eat, or when a tooth needs attention. Pain is an important part of the body system. Even emotional pain of losing a loved one, or any cherished attachment, has its place. It's straightforward. We grieve and we get over it.

The trouble comes when we assign an explanation. We blame or deny; we judge or complain. Suffering arises out of our reaction to what is, not from the underlying event or pain. That's a revelation that can set you free.

Through discrimination, through listening for the truth, we set ourselves free from suffering, not from physical pain, but from emotional suffering. If we don't become interested in the Truth, then our lives become limited to simply oscillating between our attachments and aversions.

Everyone discovers this sooner or later. This poem, in Zen-like economy, invites you to explore this within your own life to determine whether it's true.

Pain versus Suffering
4-12-06

Pain occurs in the body
It just happens
It's part of the system design
But suffering is all in the mind

Suffering comes
By adding a story to the pain

Check it out !

Commentary: Paradise

We enter paradise one by one, as we release resistance and begin saying "Yes" to Life. No one can force you to give up control or domination, but those two rascals lock you out of joy. Joy is life moving through you without resistance. When you say "yes" to life, to the flow of energy, to the circumstances that arise, you allow life's movement through you. That is joy.

Two forces are at play here: energy and resistance. If you are allowing and have high energy you experience joy. If you are allowing and have low energy, you have mild contentment. If you have high resistance and high energy, you experience negative emotions, like anger or rage. If you have resistance and low energy, then you generate a mild frustration.

If you say "No" to Life, you turn joy into negative emotion. The white alchemist knows that energy becomes joy when it is allowed to flow. The black alchemist turns joy into anger, freedom into bondage and bliss into suffering.

In *Paradise* I am suggesting you give the gift of Life back to the Giver. In the highest sense, you are the Giver; your Divine Nature is Life. So offering Life back to the Giver becomes an act of saying "Yes" to your own Divine Essence.

Paradise
9-20-07

Paradise is
Experiencing Life in joy

You are here
To live in paradise
First, find that paradise within
Then will you discover it outside

Paradise is found
By saying YES to Life
By having
No-resistance to the Truth

All Life is Her Life
You are Her ear
Her mouth
Her heart

Offer the gift
Back to the Giver
And be lifted
Into paradise

Hallelujah or Heresy?

It was not so long ago when people were persecuted for speaking like this, for suggesting that YOU and God are One — or at least, are not separate. Now this truth is being sung from the rooftops of the western world.

There may still be those, however, who would call this blasphemy and prefer to condemn and punish any outcropping of Oneness, than to open to love.

It is a tragedy that for so long our three great western traditions punished those who suggested that they were not separate from God. Jesus was condemned for suggesting "The Father and I are one." Islam has a long history of stoning anyone who spoke such blasphemy. Christianity has also suffered its dark times of murder, inquisition and witch burning.

Those times are behind us now. The dark yuga is over. It is a joy that this non-separate perspective of Oneness and unity is returning to the world and can now be written and spoken freely. This is the great good news — you are not separate from God.

I am happy that the good news is flourishing and glad to be a part of the choir, adding my perspective to the mix.

You Came Here for Your Wings
5-3-09

You came here to get your power
To get your wings, so that you might fly
Not the power of a false self, dominating the world
But the power that lives, as your Soul

Your Essential Nature is your seat of power
To move seamlessly through the dimensions
You must culture this power
You must learn to vessel your Divine Nature

You are learning to harness the power of creation
The power of mind, the power of God

Mastery is becoming the Soul, the Divine Person
So that the body-mind is in service
To your Divine Nature
If the mind coops the power in service of ego or the
Body kidnaps you into its addictions, then you suffer

That is what the "crushing" is all about, your
Unwillingness to let your Divine Nature run the show

Commentary: If Only

One of our early presidents said, "People are about as happy as they make up their mind to be." That is a great truth. How many times have you heard the statement: "If only . . . (so and so) . . . I would be happy."

This poem is a statement to say it's deeper than that. Unhappiness is embedded in the nature of the disconnected mind. We can fill in the blank forever, generate as much content as imaginable, but unhappiness dogs us. Why?

Because until you show up as the witnessing presence, the mind experiences separation. The mind is calling out to YOU to show up and command it, as its creator, but you have gotten lost inside it. It will serve you, but until you show up, it will dominate and tyrannize you. It will throw you into the dungeon of thought and leave you there.

But here is the secret, my friend: your dungeon door is not locked. The mind cannot lock the door; it can only entrance you. You may leave any time, by leaving thought and entering the present moment with awareness. Poof !!! It's that easy, and that hard.

If Only
1-10-2000

You think

If only I could change my life, I would be happy
If only I made more money or had him or her
If only I had what I wanted, I would be happy

Not so!

Unhappiness is not content-driven
It's deeper
Unhappiness is embedded
In the disconnected mind

Commentary: Visoka

I adore this poem. When the prakash moves through you, there are just no words to describe it. I have written so often about this that I am in jeopardy of becoming a one-song band. *Visoka* is bliss light.

The first three stanzas are an outpouring of that bliss light when I had a pen in my hand. I wasn't sure the poem was going anywhere. It was headed towards being just a big tub of love light.

Then, the poem turned sacred. The fourth stanza reveals one of the pure secrets of life; this sweetness is reserved for those who love. The metaphor of finding your knees came as a way to indicate becoming authentic, sincere and humble.

The final lines reveal the keys to the Mother's wine cellar. You cannot enter without the code. The code is vibrational. The lower frequencies do not have access to Her paradise until they return to innocence.

Visoka

9-8-08

The Friend is here. I am breathing Her breath
Her bliss at Being is my ever-overflowing wine cup
 This goes on as She breathes me
As He breathes me, as She breathes me

Visoka is Her name
Bliss is Her nature
Pouring out on a thirsty world

Dust becomes love particles
Water becomes Light
Sound makes love to the ears

She reserves this hidden sweetness
For those who love
 When you find your knees
You become Her darling

This is Her wonderful wine-house
 But you cannot enter — without humility
You cannot drink — without innocence
You cannot become intoxicated — without devotion

Commentary: Roos O Shab

There are many poems like this in the book echoing this song, the song of the open heart, the song of this River of Wine. Intellectuals just have no idea how delicious the open heart is. They are tasting the fruit of the mind.

When Love flows through you, when bliss moves in your veins, when your heart is openness itself and God is whispering in your ear like a lover, then you have found Her River of Wine.

Roos O Shab means night and day in Farsi. It captures the impassioned moment of calling out in ecstasy, in delight, in rapture at the sweetness of the Divine Nature flowing through. The mind is overwhelmed. The body is useless. The Ka body is in pure ecstasy endurance, asking "How long can I cook in this frequency before exploding?"

Yes, the divine path is worth traveling, soooo very worth traveling.

Roos O Shab
4-4-08

Night and day
Night and day
Always You
Night and day

This sweetness
I cannot stop drinking this sweetness

I stand beneath Your waterfall
Mouth wide open
Pouring out from You . . .this sweetness ! ! !

Oh thinkers and intellectuals
Skeptics and doubters
If you had any idea how sweet
Is the open heart

You would have abandoned your thinking years ago
And rushed headlong into this river of wine

Commentary: How Did We Get This Far?

This poem starts out as a lover's question, "How did we get this far?" We had been together for six years and we were getting underneath some deep issues. We were marveling how we had come this far. Oh yes — love!!! We had stayed in love. As we built our house and gardens, we called it 'The Love Project' because we only worked on it when we felt connected and loving, not out of duty and obligation.

As I reviewed our commitment to love the poem deepens, recognizing that it was not so much my love or her love, but Love itself.

With the words, "We are lifting ourselves out of separation into remembrance," the poem moves into deeper water. Love moves us towards remembrance. Love is non-resistance to the Truth and remembrance is self-realization. It is remembering who you are.

Then forgiveness enters as the path back to innocence — releasing judgment, resistance and separation. Innocence is openness to what is, non-resistance to the Truth.

How Did We Get This Far?
3-26-06

How did we get this far?
By loving and adoring,
By surrendering and doing the work
My job is to let you love me

Your job is to let me love you
This loving is the gift we give each other
But really, we are lifting ourselves
Out of separation into remembrance

Remembering who we were
Before the Fall
Before the descent into separation
Before we became an "I"

Forgiveness is the work
Unconditional and radical forgiveness
How else will we return to innocence?
How else will we forgive our selves
For falling asleep and imagining we were separate?

Ten Insights

"The mind needs healing — but why? What's so important about healing the mind?

1st Insight

The mind goes with you from life to life! That's a big deal — because it says you don't start over with a blank slate, a tabula rasa, but with the canvas you were painting on in your previous life.

That should give you reason to pause, because "as in the mind, so in the person." What is in your mind either binds you or liberates you. When the patterns of perception which distort the mind are stilled, then union with the Sacred Self is realized. Otherwise, one's life reflects the distortions.

The Split Mind: The mind is split into two compartments, the conscious and the unconscious. The conscious mind is not aware of what goes on in its unconscious half. It is split off from itself; that's why it is unconscious.

The conscious mind is our individual lens of perception; the holder of our beliefs and attitudes. It perceives the data coming from the senses. It is the mind that thinks, and in thinking, imagines it's in control, but it is split and does not recognize that above it rests the unconscious mind, the repository and sum total of our repressions, fears and passions, anything that was too intense to experience or was too challenging to our idea-self, our self image. This has been well understood for over 100 years by western psychology.

The Individual Unconscious: The individual unconscious is where our individual denials and repressions are stored, from this life and all our other lives. Whatever we have been unable or unwilling to experience is stored here awaiting resolution, and this is where the problem lies. These threads of energy, coming from the shadows, flow into the conscious mind and influence it; they distort it, and it all happens in plain view, but the conscious mind is oblivious. It doesn't have a clue what is going on. That is the quandary of the split mind.

The split mind is Dr. Jekyll [conscious mind] and Mr. Hyde [unconscious mind] at work. The conscious mind is fine – until the repressions within the unconscious mind project into its world and an obstacle appears, an uncontrollable anger, a pain body attack. Hyde has arrived, the evil twin. The work of recognizing these projections is sometimes called "shadow work" in psychology because they appear to arise from the shadows, out of nowhere. The unconscious is essentially bleeding into the conscious mind creating all manner of distortion.

2nd Insight

The unconscious mind is what veils the Spiritual Light. The unconscious mind acts as a barrier to seeing or remembering the Light. It is the blindfold, the veil, the reason we can't perceive who we really are or where we came from. The unconscious mind feels like an ocean of dreams.

3rd Insight

The unconscious mind is not linear like the conscious mind; it is timeless. Two minutes or a thousand years can be the same; seeds are seeds. Seeds are unresolved issues. Life invokes unresolved seed issues seeking release and resolution. When we deal with them correctly, we integrate the resulting realization into our wisdom. If not, then we rely upon past patterns to deal with them, and the issues persist.

These unresolved impressions travel with us from life to life, re-expressing when conditions are right. This is karma. If we don't transform it, we are condemned to relive it. Not out of punishment, but out of the desire of the Soul to heal itself, to resolve those issues pushed down into unconsciousness. The Soul seeks wholeness, not a split mind filled with repressions.

4th Insight

Resolution is achieved by experiencing whatever arises consciously, allowing the feeling to be felt and integrated, blessed, and released. If forgiveness is required, then forgive. If release is required, then release. However don't stop there. The all important action step must be taken. Issues don't fully resolve themselves until we act on our realization. It is action that creates actualization converting head knowledge into wisdom.
Spiritual work is not about making us well-adjusted members of society by showing us how

to suppress or circumvent Mr. Hyde; that is the job that psychology has taken on – to make us functional human beings in our society. Spiritual work is about emptying the unconscious of its distortions. We want to empty the unconscious so that it is no longer a barrier.

The Collective Unconscious: :   Above the individual unconscious mind exists the collective unconscious. This is the aspect of mind Jung identified and popularized. We all share this mind together. It holds our collective agreements and perceptions. It has similar qualities to the individual unconscious, but it is archetypal and universal and vast. It too is a sea of dreams.

5th Insight

Divine Mind: Above the collective unconscious lies Divine Mind. Given names like Christ Mind, Buddha Mind, Paramahamsa Caitanya [Sanskrit] or the Super Conscious, it is the seat of all wisdom and knowledge and is shared collectively by all. This is where individuation returns to Source, where the individual fingers merge into the one hand. It is from here that mystics make statements like "The Father and I are one.". They are simply speaking the truth from the Mind of God, the Divine Mind.

Everyone would like to have access to Divine Mind, if they knew of it. Who wouldn't want to know what *really* happened in the past – first hand by your own perception, or what might happen in the future, or what the truth is in the moment, how to heal illness, or what might happen in the markets? The ability to access Divine Mind is an unbelievable, unfathomable gift. The ego goes crazy speculating about all the wonderful things it could amass for itself. However, we are blocked by the individual and collective unconscious mind. The ego cannot get through the field of dreams. The conscious mind cannot just prance in and snatch the grail; it gets snared in the dream. To move from the conscious mind to the Super Conscious mind, this ocean must be crossed.

6th Insight

Atma-Prakash: Above Divine Mind is Atma-Prakash, the pure Life-Creating Light. Light is an expression of Spirit. It floods into the created worlds sustaining all things. It is Life. It is aliveness.

7th Insight

In order to heal the mind or traverse the worlds, the unconscious mind must be stilled, the distortions resolved, the barriers removed. That is what healing the mind means. Then the Light can shine into the conscious mind. We become illuminated – by the Light, which is Spirit made manifest.

Healing the Mind: It's not so easy to heal the unconscious mind. Belief systems, which is what it is made up of, don't touch it. Improving attitudes, while wonderful and life affirming, doesn't touch it. Fasting, praying, penance, confessions, vision quests – none of them go deep enough to transform the unconscious. Behaving, having a positive attitude, following the rules, going to church, temple, or mosque, being a good person, doing good works, none of these go deep enough. These activities can prevent us from adding to the unconscious, and in that, they are wonderful and life-affirming; however, transforming the unconscious takes something special. It requires a deep tool.

How do we heal the mind? Where do we find that deep tool?
1]   Do the spiritual work
2]   Flood the body with Light, the Prakash Light from above the super conscious Divine Mind.

8th Insight

Doing 'The Work':   We start the work by recognizing and acknowledging the influence of the split mind, the projections and distortions flowing into awareness from the unconscious. They can form as much as 80 percent of conscious reality. Own them. Admit to yourself that the aberrations you experience are coming courtesy of your own unconscious mind. Become a student of what you think, say and do. Become very interested in what is moving through you. Stop blaming. Take the position that if it happened to you, then somehow, in some mysterious, yet to be discovered way, you had a hand in it. That is the mind set for doing the work.

9th Insight

Forgive your transgressors: yes they behaved badly; no doubt about that, but it is you who cast them and drew them to you to help you, one more time, to release buried material. So get busy and release it, whatever it is. Don't waste time blaming. Yes someone did you wrong; get over it. Blaming just keeps your unconscious loaded with insanity. Get on with your real work.

Forgive that person — and not from 'noble' forgiveness, not from the forgiveness that says, "Okay, I'll be noble and forgive you." NO! That is not deep enough; noble forgiveness does not shift the underlying ground of being. It stays put. Forgive from the place that says, "I forgive you, because it has probably been me that acted in this same way towards others, in some forgotten past. I forgive you and I forgive myself." That is radical forgiveness. That frees you. It unhooks you from the unconscious.

Compassion can be even more elegant than forgiveness. Forgiveness assumes a wrong. Compassion doesn't. Radical forgiveness has the wisdom to say, "I too have transgressed." Compassion embodies humility which says "I don't really know what is right for another person and I am open to hear what is right for me. I'm not sure if a wrong was committed." This deep "a-ha" realization contained within humility allows you to move forward without anyone having to be wrong.

All you need is your awareness, your mindfulness, owning it all, forgiving it all, and finding compassion. That will unhook you. A lifetime of such practice will go a long way towards freeing you.

10th Insight

<u>Atma-Prakash</u>:   The mind can be healed through flooding the etheric body, the light body, the Ka, with Atma-Prakash, the pure Life-Creating Light. Atma-Prakash increases the vibration in the Ka body and ushers in radiance. The nadis, the etheric equivalent of the meridians, are filled with light and vibration. The Life-Creating Light does the healing. The frequency in the light body, the Ka, begins to increase. At some point, an alchemy occurs; instead of drawing its energy from the environment through food, water, air and exercise, the Ka begins feeding directly from the spiritual Light.

How to actually accomplish this can be learned through Sambodha (www.sambodha.org). The practices have been brought directly from the vault of all knowledge, the Nabho Ghano Akash, through Aaravindha's saumedhika sight. An entire body of sacred wisdom has been assembled within Sambodha from the vault of Divine Mind. We have this knowledge because Aaravindha has been willing to use his gift for humanity.

He is reintroducing the ancient methods taught by the immortal masters to create illumination and ascension. It involves Pavana meditations, a method of activating the divine meridian, the nadis, and cleansing the unconscious mind.

Commentary: Pavana

Pavanas are an evolution beyond kriyas, an ailiyana, literally meaning the Breath of God. Pavanas "order" the elements within the physiology, fill the meridians with pure *shakti*, raise consciousness toward realization and heal the mind. Pavanas are a gift from the Solar Lineage.

Pavana meditation works with energy (*shakti*), light (*prakash*), sound (*nada*), and the divine language (*mantra*).

Pavanas use the inherent sacred pathways within our own physiology to enliven the *Devatapratima*, the divine prototype that rests at the source of the human form, or what could be called Tree of Life. This ultimately heals the mind through opening the inner pathways to Light.

With practice, the inner meridians and vibrational channels are opened to the Light flooding down into the body from the crown. You become radiant. Mantra leads awareness into silence. Mindfulness develops.

Frequency broadcasts through silence ignites *shakti* in the meridians. Heartfulness is cultured. The mind is cleansed of obscuring elements by the Shine of Consciousness.

"Once initiated into the pavanas, the devotee will be capable of developing in a way that was not possible for many thousands of years. At this point, the level of practice already exceeds anything else available at this time. These techniques are the missing link. What has made ascension nearly impossible for most of the dark Yuga is eradicated through these practices."

Paradise is found

By saying YES to Life

Paradise, pg 259

Pavana
4-28-08

Oh sacred sounds
You have slaughtered me again
Like a drunk in the garden
Swooning

I had no idea
That sound could do this
That frequency would open
The nectar door

My whole being is filled with sweetness
I am floating in a sea of honey

My Soul is drunk
My heart is open
My body full of bliss

This Love field is cooking me
As I willingly drown
In this endless swelling gratitude

Commentary: Mantra

Mantras are subtle frequencies. They are derivations of the divine language, the angelic language, which is not a spoken language, but a vibrational language. They already exist in your consciousness.

Mantra leads to silence. It is a process of becoming subtler and subtler. At first, mantra might be spoken aloud, so it seats in the mind. But as you speak it ever softer and softer, it vibrates only in the mind becoming barely audible. As you deepen still further, it is no longer even pronounced within the mind, but is simply an essential vibration.

That is a subtle distinction to investigate, becoming aware of the difference between words being pronounced quietly in the mind and pure thought. It becomes pure intention, an impulse. The following poem attempts to communicate this intimate experience of deepening. What is vibrating on the deepest level, is YOU.

If you can learn to speak this language of the gods, you can set yourself free.

Mantra
8-15-07

YOU are the reed
That vibrates
Tones do not happen "through you"
But "as you"

YOU are what vibrates

You are the flute
And the holes in the flute
And the air
Moving through

Breath moves
Through Itself
To become sound
You are that sound dancing

Commentary: Why Do You Weep?

I call it "being moved". Pentecostals might call it anointing. The heart swells, warm tears come flooding down the cheeks, but it is not sentimental, not emotional. It is not the personality or the mind that is involved. It is the descent of Spirit upon the flesh.

It feels as if the Soul is plunging Itself into me, into the body, into the heart. As if a downward facing triangle sat above, tip to tip, with an upward facing triangle below and the triangle above was somehow the Spirit and It plunged downward into the lower triangle, representing the body-mind, until it looked like the Star of David — two triangles resting within each other.

I can't function when this happens. It overwhelms me. All I can do is weep. It is probably why we incarnate with only a fraction of our radiance. If the Soul fully entered the body with the full luminescence of its Love, it would fry every circuit in the body.

Why Do You Weep?
5-2-08

These tears come
As Hafiz opens my Soul with his gentle hand
As Rumi dazzles my heart with dancing
My face again runs wet

Why do I weep? you ask
Because when the Soul hears the Truth
In this dusty outpost, and remembers
What it was like before the Fall
Before it said "yes" to separation

It remembers who it is !

That remembering cracks this world open, and
For a moment, paradise is birthed
The Soul trembles at the impact
Of remembering how beautiful this world is
If only . . . if only . . . we brought Love

Tears are that remembering

Commentary: You Are What Is

When enough sleep leaves our eyes, when enough
separation has slipped away, when we finally
get it, when it finally dawns on us that "We are
It", we relax into the universe. We are what IS.
Hallelujah!

I like the metaphor of sugar dissolving in water,
for ego dissolving in the Divine, because the sugar
is still there, the sweetness is still there. It has
changed forms. It is now in solution, rather than
granular. That's a perfect metaphor.

The ego still functions. I still know the difference
between my arm and yours. Just perfect, Oneness
with distinctions within it.

Everyone will one day remember the truth. This
poem acknowledges that sacred remembering.

You Are What Is
10-2-2000

As the ego
Approaches the Divine
It dissolves
Like sugar in water

The personality
Dissolves into Self
You discover you are not who you thought you were
You are a vastness without measure

You are love without equal
You discover you are, what is

Commentary: What is Now

When enough fog leaves our mind that we begin to perceive directly what is, rather than through the lens of mental reference, then the present moment takes on a magical quality. It becomes the place where everything happens.

This poem arose out of a revelation that came rolling through for months. It felt like the moment itself was the Soul, that the eternal moment WAS the Soul. Perhaps because that is where direct perception occurs and awareness is self aware.

What is Now
6-26-2000

The present moment
IS your Soul
Directly experiencing life

There is no you
That has this Soul
There's just That

If you stay in your mind
You'll miss it all

Commentary: Divine Meridian

The next two poems are about my experience with the practices of Sambodha, Aaravindha's teaching community.

The five elements in the body are harmonized and the spiritual technology in the head is activated. The result is a growing radiance, self-realization and a healed mind. The lens of perception is cleared for direct seeing. The ability to hear the truth is cultured and the force field around the body is strengthened to resist negativity, especially our own.

The *Divine Meridian* is the name for the Tree of Life as it extends down through the body. These practices ignite the tree. I wrote this poem after eight months of practice. The internal conductivity, which at first seemed mechanical, turned to bliss within the first year of practice.

Divine Meridian
9-5-07

Divine meridian
Blissful pathway
The body purrs
Smiles, purrs again

Up and down
The divine meridian
Each kriya
Intoxicating

Each MA
Holy relaxation
Each NG
Oceanic

Why so much pleasure?
It was not this way in the beginning
But now — oh my
It goes on, and I do not want to stop

Commentary: Stargate

I use the term stargate, because it has become popular in movies and is now understood as a portal between dimensions. Just such technology exists in your head and your etheric body or what the Egyptians called the Ka Body.

The practices of Sambodha stem from an ancient tradition, which teaches how to harness this inner world to guide ourselves towards self-realization and beyond.

I consider this to be the most advanced approach to the deeper levels of God Realization on the planet today.

Stargate
1-14-09

What if I told you that there is a stargate
Hidden in the crown of your head?
A portal between worlds, the gateway to
 "The Kingdom", closer to you than your own nose?
Would you be interested in such a journey?

The corridor lies between the pineal gland
And the crown of your head
It is so unknown in the west
There isn't even a name for it in English

But it is there waiting for you
To become interested in the adventure
The ancients called it the Brahmarandra Nadi
The stairway to Heaven

It moves between your individuality
And your non-local Self
Open it and you are flooded with light
It is your birthright to travel this road any time you want.

The only cost, "Check your ego at the door"

Commentary: The Blue Star Mother

This is a love poem to the Blue Star Mother. She is one of the living masters of the Solar Lineage. During a seminar in Semiahmoo, Aaravindha told about his meeting with these masters. He mentioned their names. When he spoke Her name, a flood of energy passed through me.

I knew I could reach through time and connect with Her. I laid my head back and silently called out to Her and she became absolutely present — energetically. I said I was ready and to please show me the way. Life has not been the same since.

This poem expresses my inability not to adore her, love her, thank her, and be playful.

The Blue Star Mother
12-10-07

Thank you, thank you, thank you! ! !
For bringing me home

When I opened to you, I had no idea
When we met, how could I have known?
My heart singing to your heart
I had no idea who you were

But my Heart did. It knew to call on You
It knew to open. It knew to surrender without condition
Now, you have entered and made love with my Soul
You tear away at my ignorance, fill me with Light

This bliss, this radiance
This love for everyone and everything
This constant spilling over

I open my heart; you fill it with love
I ask a question; you put the answer in my mouth
I summon you; love overwhelms me
Now, even my foolishness wants to come see you

Commentary:: Where Are My Priests

When I heard the Divine Mother say, "Where are my priests?" my heart leapt up and shouted "I am your priest. I am your priest."

My connection with her had already been established and she was an energetic reality for me. To be connected to an immortal, like the Blue Star Mother, and under her tutelage was a blessing.

Earlier in my life I had been saved from war by the immortal Babaji, the founder of the SRF tradition. I knew the potency of such beings and I was feeling gratitude to have a second chance to be under their guidance and direction through the connection with Aaravindha and his Sambodha mystery school.

So when I heard her call, I leapt to my feet. I am your priest, my heart shouted. I am your priest. Use me too, to do your work. That was my hearts call — use me also to do your work.

Where Are My Priests
10-6-07

"Where are my priests"?
She asks

Beloved, I am your priest
I am your hands
Your mouth
Your eyes

Let us dance this love-wisdom
To our hungry world

These hands were born for this
These eyes, made for this
This mouth was formed, just for this
My Heart has fallen to its knees yearning for this

Let us nourish our people
With true Self knowledge
Let us throw open the door to God
And walk hand in hand into paradise

Commentary:: The Last Hurdle

If you can let the mind go completely — for just a moment — and feel what is present — actually present in the moment — the luminous, aware, life force that is the mysterious you — you can move into a moment of direct recognition. To do this, you have to get out of your mind. Letting go of your concept of God can do this. You can always pick it up again at the door.

Can you get a sense of it, a feeling, an impulse?

There can be a magical moment of direct innocent perception. You can study for years and not have such a moment, but if you let go of your concept of God and relax into the here and now moment, feeling into what is present, such a moment may be yours. This poem takes a stab at creating such a moment for you. Remove a concept — experience the reality.

For those of you taking a big gulp, relax; it is safe to let the concept go. It was useful, but it's a concept; the reality of God is elsewhere. The reality is not going to disappear because you release the concept. You are releasing a concept so that you can go beyond mind and experience the reality.

The Last Hurdle
5-3-09

After presence
After allowing
After compassion
After nirodha

The final hurdle!
Releasing the CONCEPT of God
Let it go — it's only in the mind
Go meet the reality without your concept

Now . . . what's left?
What is here in this moment
Looking out your eyes?
The YOU, beyond the mind?

The concept was usefull, absolutely
The pole star of a lifetime
But now you have crossed the river
Leave the boat behind

Travel on, as your Self

Commentary: The Yoga of Light

Yoga of Light is an outpouring of gratitude.
The territory beyond silence was finally open.
Hallelujah! I had meditated for nearly 40 years,
in silence for nearly 20 years, and spent the last
5 years knowing in my bones that there was more
to it than silence, more to it than even stillness, yet
not knowing what that "more" was.

But no one was talking about this. Everyone I
knew, from Ramana Maharshi to Papaji, Gangaji
to Adyashanti were praising silence and stillness.
And indeed, silence and stillness were magnificent,
monumental, remarkable and fundamentally
required, but my knowingness told me this was
not the end of the path. There was more. Then the
blessing came — and the door opened.

Yoga of Light tells the story of how the call to move
beyond silence arrived, the discovery of radiance,
meeting the immortal Blue Star Mother, and the
recognition that I was home.

It is a rampage of appreciation for my friend and
mentor, Aaravindha.

Yoga of Light
10-4-07

Thank you Aaravindha
The radiance has been flowing for months now
But today, I recognized it
I realized it

This high frequency, deeply rooted, felt luminous-ness
Different than peace
Different than happiness
Different than bliss

I saw it in you
During the months we worked together on the office
I saw that you were living luminously

It wasn't really happiness, yet you were happy
It wasn't positive-ness, yet you were positive
It wasn't bliss, yet you were blissful

I know lots of people who live positively
And that's a beautiful quality
I know people who are happy

CONTINUED >>

And that too is magnificent
But radiance is its own gift
Distinct unto itself, an effulgent luminous joy
Radiating through the energy body
A quiet swelling joy

What a grace — thank you

There have been sooooo many blessings
For fifteen years I had been Ramana's kid
He somehow showed me the Self
He passed on the gift of recognition

The Self soooo enjoys Itself
For years the bliss of recognition
Flowed quietly in the background
An unending enjoyment of Its Own Nature

Yet I was called from silence
The Mother began whispering so softly in my ear
"Sweetheart, now that you are awake
WHAT IS POSSIBLE? "

I was called back into Life: I built a house
I loved a woman
I studied the positive
I became abundant

Then my ancient roots came calling
In the person of Aaravindha
"Yogata Prakash," you said, the Yoga of Light
The Divine Science of Enlightenment

I was ripped from my moorings
From my focus on house and garden
From my sweet lover
From my consuming

So gently, so lovingly, yet so inexorably
Was I called to this Light
I could see the Beloved's hand everywhere
Shaping my life

You had just returned from the valley
Three weeks with the masters
Now spilling out your adventure with us

CONTINUED >>

You named them all, and as you spoke
Her name, the Blue Star Mother
Something exploded

She called out to me
I called out to Her
Somewhere we met
Somewhere I opened

You gave me Her
She gave me you
All year we have been dancing

The Devi Bhut Atmaka
The Light Regeneration Meditation

The Science of Mind Intensive
The Mahantarapatha Pavanas
The Blue Medicine Mantra
The Chakra Intensive
Sailing together through Grizzly Bears
Wiring your office

I began noticing this constant RADIANCE
A quiet, gentle effulgence
Friends too began noticing
Acknowledging the Shine

My friends asked, "How are you, Sonjan?"

"On fire," I replied, "flying down the face of the twelve foot wave of my life with all ten toes hanging over the nose, hair on fire and shouting for pure exhilarating joy of it. Out of control, radiantly happy, just perfect."

"Why do you think that is?" they asked.

That evening, while reading the Saumedhika sutras, it leaped off the page and I knew how radiance had arrived.

"Once initiated into the Pavanas, the devotee will be capable of developing in a way that was not possible for many thousands of years. At this point, the level of practice already exceeds anything else available at this time. These techniques are the missing link. What has made ascension nearly impossible for most of the dark Yuga is eradicated through these practices."

Aaravindha Himadra: Born with a Gift
by Sonjan

Aaravindha Himadra was born with a gift. He was born a rishi, a seer. He has had access to the Divine Mind since birth. There is so little known about this skill in the west, that for years he simply called it "The Oracle". Now he uses the old Sanskrit term *saumedhika* sight. A facet of the *sahasrara* (crown chakra) opens giving access to Divine Mind. All human beings have this chakra — Aaravindha's is open.

For most of us, we listen and discern. For Aaravindha, he softens his gaze and "seeing" occurs. The vault of time opens and he perceives backwards and forwards in time/space. The ancients of India knew of this skill and cultivated it, calling it access to *Nabogana Akash,* the vault of all knowledge. Until you live around someone who has this skill, it is impossible to imagine the enormity of the gift.

Aaravindha comes from a line of masters, known as the Solar Lineage. These sages are his people. This is his lineage. In 2006 he was invited by the immortal masters to come to the valley. He trekked there and spent almost a month with them, the first westerner to do so in almost 100 years.

The only knowledge we have of them, in the public record, comes from the Self Realization Fellowship line, through the story of Babaji, the immortal master, founder of Kriya Yoga. They are the keepers of a knowledge so old even our myths don't go back that far, and so powerful that death has been transcended.

Aaravindha is reintroducing their techniques to humanity. He is offering this treasure to you.

Website: www.sambodha.org.

The Key to Enlightenment
by Aaravindha

There is an absolute silent Self. But within that silent Self, there is an infinite and undying creativity. Some would say that only that Self is real — whereas the fact is that also everything that is within that Self, and that is the expression of its life, then must also be real — even though in its parts we can't see its entire nature. So we cast away the part in order to find the whole, but in casting away the parts, we have denied the whole.

Many believe that we must break away from the wheel of samsara, that we must break away from wheel of rebirth and enter this state of re-merging with God. Where is that going to take place, that merging with God? Where exactly is God right now?

This question has to be answered, because many paths suggest that you must achieve your enlightenment and you must overcome or transcend life and be able to merge back with the perfect blissful Self that is God. And that in itself is a neutralization of their own effort.

First, pursuit is a statement of separation. Second, if you are going to merge with God and God is all there is, then this is already God. There is nothing to merge with. So there are two aspects of that pursuit path that become some of the greatest obstacles to the awakening of all. That is the idea that we are somehow going to improve upon something that is already perfect by its own nature. We look for the perfection, but the mind will never see it. It is not intent for the mind to see perfection, because the perfection is absolute. It is timeless. It is whole. But within it, exist all the ripples of potential that make up this universe and all the other universes and that is essential to it.

There is a reason for Life. And that reason is, very simply, God wants to BE. That underlying fundamental perfection of consciousness, that radiance, that Shine, wants to be.

When the One became aware of itself, it created a relationship out of the one, it had two, and out of that two, the one wanting to know itself, infinite potential began to flow forward and that became Life. Suddenly we had the birth of the universe. And that is in an order; it is the story; it is the answer.

The One said Who? The One said THIS. It has never stopped talking THIS, and will never stop talking this. Life is an infinite potential. This is the point that needs to be understood within the reach and scope of enlightenment. Infinite is forever. It's eternal everlasting life. Everlasting Life, in a timeless foundation, shoreless, eternal foundation.

Now, the key is not to achieve the eternal. We already have it. We already have the infinite. The key to enlightenment is to learn how to live within it; how to be in a state of nonresistance so that we can hear the divine intention that is the One in a state of nonresistance to the One. Give up all resistance to the perfect order, to the perfect Shine that is being revealed to the self.

When the barriers, the shadows and the illusions are dissolved, what remains is the Light. However that Light is not an emptiness; it's a fullness, an absolute fullness that will never cease revealing its perfection. If there is no resistance to the Light, that experience is a state of being that can only be called love — no resistance to the Truth.

When there is no resistance to the Light of the Self, when all the shadows have been removed, a creative expression is allowed to flow through the mind. The mind becomes a vehicle for the expression of God's will. That becomes the dharma, the purpose, the reason for you living, and that purpose then becomes that which carries you into the Sun, into the full light of your reason for being. That is the moment you take birth. That is the beginning of your life, not the end of it.

It is not merging back into God; it's the realization that God has always been all there is — and that everything is resting in the sweetness of God's love. Everything! And to give into that love; to fall in love again and again — and to be grateful for this little tiny bit of illusion of separation that we might have the opportunity to have relationship — and to abandon the heart to that, to fall into that love without hesitation or resistance.

Glossary of Terms

Aaravindha: American born mystic, saumedhika seer, founder of Sambodha.

Adipavana: the first of the pavanas taught in Aaravindha's Sambodha wisdom school involving the initial tones of the sacred Mahantarapatha Meditation.

Advaita: non-dual or "not two".

Amartya: immortal master.

Antara'Pavana: the internal Sun Tones; the third pavana taught in the Sambodha tradition.

Arka Vamsha: ancient name for the Solar Lineage.

Babaji: an immortal amartya master, founder of Kriya Yoga.

Beloved: an affectionate name for God.

Bhakti: devotion.

Blue Star Mother: a living immortal amartya master of the Solar Lineage living in the Himalayas.

Book of Maat: ancient wisdom book of the secrets of the universe withdrawn from this world during the fall into the dark yuga. Her wisdom is now re-emerging.

Brahmarandra Nadi: God's channel or meridian, resting between the Ajna chakra and the Sahasrara Chakra.

Creation Field: a field of time/space where thoughts held in consciousness create reality.

Coleman Barks: an American poet, renowned as an interpreter of Rumi.

Daniel Ladinsky: an American poet, renowned as an interpreter of Hafiz.

Dharma: our divinely intended path through life.

Dhyana: meditation; awareness without thought; Patanjali's seventh stage of Raja Yoga.

Divine Mind: the mind that rests above the human mind; the mind of God; Christ mind.

Divine Essence: Spirit.

Divine Nature: Spirit.

Divine Meridian: the sushumna; the central channel through the spine in the subtle body running from the crown in the cranium to the perineum at the base of the spine.

Divine Language: Devangari, the angelic language; a non-spoken language of vibration.

Devatapratima: the image of God; the Divine prototype for all beings.

Devi'Bhut'Atmaka: a profound and powerful spiritual exercise used to bring quintessential healing and order to oneself and the universe.

Divine Qualities: non-ego based qualities which emanate from Spirit, such as love and gratitude.

Dissolution: the idea that the individual self or soul disappears or dissolves completely in God and loses all individual attributes and existence, reflected in the popular metaphor of the drop entering the Ocean.

Duality: creation; includes the third dimensional universe, and the upper worlds which maintain a semblance of separation.

(the) Friend: a Sufi reference to God.

Dogen: Zen master and gifted poet who lived in Japan during the early 1200's.

Embracing: the antithesis of pivoting; facing the issue, the thought or feeling, and embracing it, feeling it, and inhabiting it — fully feeling it with undefended awareness. The power of consciousness acts as a solvent to dissolve all frequencies lower than Itself. Divine qualities thrive while ego-based emotions dissolve in a field of presence, which is what embracing creates.

Essential Nature: Spirit.

Hafiz: Sufi poet of the 1300's in Persia.

Herself: refers to God in the feminine aspect.

I Am presence: Spirit.

Jeshua: Jesus of Nazareth; his actual Aramaic name: Jeshua Ben Joseph.

Ka Body: Egyptian name for the subtle body, energy body, etheric body.

Klesha: a vulnerability that allows unconscious negative patterns to express.

Kriya Yoga: a form of enlightenment practice taught to Lahiri Mahasaya in the 1800's by Babaji, an immortal amartya master. Yogananda popularized Kriya Yoga in the west in the early 20th century and founded the Self Realization Fellowship. As Yogananda describes Kriya Yoga, "The Kriya Yogi mentally directs his life energy to revolve, upward and downward, around the six spinal centers (medullary, cervical, dorsal, lumbar, sacral, and coccygeal plexuses) which correspond to the twelve astral signs of the zodiac, the symbolic Cosmic Man. One half-minute of revolution of energy around the sensitive spinal cord of man effects subtle progress in his evolution; that half-minute of Kriya equals one year of natural spiritual unfoldment."

Light: prakash, spiritual light, not capable of being seen by the human senses, but can be seen clairvoyantly in the crown of the head, or in out-of-body experiences, as in the legendary "light at the end of the tunnel" experience.

Local address: my affectionate name for the human condition; the experience of being in a body, separate from everybody else and everything else, assuming to be the subject to a world full of objects; the perspective of the ego in a body. This is in contrast to the Non-Local address, which is Spirit and transcendent in nature.

Mahantarapatha: the Internal Path of the Spiritual Sun; the highest line of Solar meditations.

(the) Mother: an affectionate name for the feminine aspect of God, in contrast to the Father.

Maat: ancient Egyptian goddess and consort to Thoth, embodying truth, balance, order, morality and justice. Her primary role in Egyptian mythology was the weighing of souls that took place in the underworld. Her feather was the measure that determined whether the souls (considered to reside in the heart) of the departed would reach the paradise of afterlife successfully.

Meditation: a state of being conscious without thought (silent), Patanjali's seventh stage of Yoga.

Mantra: sacred tones [frequencies] or syllables repeated in meditation or specific spiritual practices.

Mindfulness: a deep Buddhist concept. In popular usage today it refers to being present, aware, and receptive in the moment — mindful, in contrast to being obsessed, distracted, or lost in thought. When awareness side-steps thought, and stands purely in the here and now moment, self-aware and free of distraction, then you have "presence"— Spirit standing in itself, self aware.

The word mindfulness arose from a 1881 scholarly translation of Buddhist sutras into English; however I feel the word is a mistranslation, since it has nothing to do with the mind. Just the opposite, it is the absence of thought, akin to Patanjali's dhyana or meditation.

Non-separation: the mystical realization that all things are connected in Oneness, even though appearing distinct; all points within the field are not separate from the Field Itself; the awareness localized in the point is also part of the Field; there is but One Spirit, one Being playing all the roles.

Non-dual: not two, Advaita, not separate, unity, Oneness of all things. To say "One" implies sameness. Better to say "not two" which suggests that while things appear to be distinct, they are not separate.

Nabogana Akash: the vault of all knowledge, existing in the Akash, the etheric or subtle world.

Prakash: spiritual Light, not perceived by the five human senses.

Original Nature: Spirit.

Pavana: purificatory; a pure and holy uplifting act; a meditation practice beyond kriyas.

Padmasambhava: Buddhist monk who brought Buddhism to Tibet; the lotus born.

Pivoting: a term that has become popular in American culture to describe consciously moving your attention off a negative thought and onto to something more uplifting. Everyone has the power to do this. It is a choice. Pivoting reflects the choice to focus on the positive.

Rumi: famous Sufi mystic poet, 1207 to 1273, founder of the school of the Whirling Dervishes. Popularized in the west by Coleman Barks, Rumi is the bestselling poet in America.

Ramana Maharshi: famous sage of Arunachala in south India, 1879 to 1950. Ramana maintained that the purest form of his teachings was the powerful silence which radiated from his presence and quieted the minds of those attuned to it. He gave verbal teachings only for the benefit of those who could not understand his silence.

Ramayana: oldest holy book of India which tells of the exploits of Rama, Sita, Hanuman, etc and many prehistoric events.

Sadhu: a mystic, yogi or wandering monk solely dedicated to achieving liberation.

Samadhi: a high level altered state of consciousness; the eighth and final stage of development identified in the Yoga Sutras of Patanjali; a non-dualistic state of consciousness in which the mind has become still yet remains conscious; the consciousness of the experiencing subject becomes one with the experienced object.

Sambodha: translates as "Self-Realization" or "True Self Knowledge"; the school of wisdom founded by Aaravindha Himadra re-introducing the ancient knowledge and techniques of the immortal amartya masters [Solar Lineage] to the western world. Website: www.sambodha.org

Saraswathi: goddess of India; first of the Feminine Trinity; consort to Brahma; the White Goddess of Mantra Shakthi, wisdom, creativity and knowledge; associated with the throat and the mantra "aimng"; symbol of knowledge, music and arts.

Sarvamahat: a mantra meditation practiced in the Sambodha wisdom tradition.

Satsang: a spiritual gathering where a discourse is given.

Saumedhika sight: the ability to see into the other world through a facet of the crown chakra opening to yield conscious access to the vault of all knowledge (Nabogana Akash).

Savitri: Savitri is a character in Sri Aurobindo's Savitri, a Legend and a Symbol in which he describes the personage Savitri as "the Divine World, daughter of the Sun, goddess of the supreme Truth who comes down and is born to save." I use the word Savitri to mean one who is initiated into the Solar Lineage or one whose development is such that they listen for and embody divine intention in lieu of their own agenda.

Self: (spelled with a capital "S") is the ultimate perceiver, the Divine; the Creator, God.

self: (spelled with a small "s") is the individual person, the body-mind-ego perspective.

Self-liberation: moksha; "release" from illusion and suffering inherent in reincarnation.

Self Realization Fellowship: spiritual wisdom school founded by Paramahansa Yogananda, based on the teachings of the Amartya master, Babaji.

Shakti: Pure Goddess Power and the primordial cosmic energy, the dynamic forces that move through the entire universe. Shakti is the concept, or personification, of divine feminine creative power, sometimes referred to as "The Great Divine Mother". She births creation.

[the] Shine: another name for the Prakash, the spiritual light; the Light of God.

Silence: a state of being where mind stops thinking and mental silence is experienced; very few thoughts are occurring yet the subject is fully conscious. Silence is associated with the alpha and theta brain wave states.

Solar Lineage: an unbroken line of immortal amartya masters.

Sonjan: spiritual name for Chris McCombs, meaning gentle heart.

Spirit: God is Spirit . . . and Spirit is God. My sense of it is that Spirit is the old name for Consciousness. Consciousness carries the I Am Presence. This is discovered in meditation.

Together, consciousness and I Am are so fundamental to our description of God that nothing moves without them. Then — are they qualities of God or synonyms?

SRF: Self Realization Fellowship, founded by Paramahansa Yogananda.

Stillness: a deeper state of silence, where no thoughts arise, associated with the lower theta brain wave states.

Sufi: the mystical dimension of Islam. Sufi scholars have defined Sufism as "a science whose objective is the reparation of the heart and turning it away from all else but God."

Tjehuthi: Egyptian name for Thoth; an immortal being.

Truth Vidya Mantra: Truth Knowledge mantra; makes one fall in love with the Truth.

Truth Expanse: A timeless field of absolute truth consciousness, Satyam Rtam Bharat, the infinite expanse of the absolute whole of consciousness

[the] Transcendent: Spirit.

Yuga: a long cycle of time lasting 24,000 to 26,000 years in which the spiritual energy fluctuates from high to low and back to high. The Kali Yuga is the dark yuga at the bottom of the sequence described as a 6,000 year cycle from which we are now rising towards a golden era.

Yogananda: an Indian yogi (1893-1952) who brought Kriya Yoga and meditation to the western world; founder of Self Realization Fellowship; author of Autobiography of a Yogi.

Yoga Sutras of Patanjali: the foundational text for Yoga; an enormously influential work.

Visoka: bliss light.

Shiva: Hindu deity, one of the three aspects of God in the Hindu Trinity; the destroyer.

Vishnu: Hindu deity, one of the 3 aspects of God in the Hindu Trinity; the maintainer.

Whirling: the practice of spinning made popular by Rumi in the thirteenth century and one of the major portals to transcendent experience.

Yeshua: alternate spelling to Jeshua; Jesus of Nazareth.

Yogata Prakash: Yoga of Light; the yoga taught by the amartya masters and Aaravindha.

Vritti: a mental idea or concept; often associated with mental patterns or habits; acting like a whirlpool, a rabbit hole we unconsciously fall into over and over.

Index

CPSIA information can be obtained at www.ICGtesting.com
Printed in the USA
LVOW040401221111

255893LV00001B/2/P